Also by Catherine Kaputa

You Are a Brand (2nd edition)
Women Who Brand
Breakthrough Branding
Graduate to a Great Career

THE NEW BRAND YOU

How to Wow in the New World of Work

Catherine Kaputa

nb

NICHOLAS BREALEY
PUBLISHING

BOSTON • LONDON

First published in 2022 by Nicholas Brealey Publishing
An imprint of John Murray Press

An Hachette UK company

26 25 24 23 22   1 2 3 4 5 6 7 8 9 10

A CIP catalogue record for this title is available from the British Library

Library of Congress Control Number: 2022933577

ISBN 978-1-3998-0406-6
US eBook ISBN 978-1-3998-0409-7
UK eBook ISBN 978-1-3998-0408-0

Printed and bound in the United States of America.

John Murray Press policy is to use papers that are natural, renewable, and
recyclable products and made from wood grown in sustainable forests. The logging
and manufacturing processes are expected to conform to the environmental
regulations of the country of origin.

John Murray Press Ltd
Carmelite House
50 Victoria Embankment
London EC4Y 0DZ
Tel: 020 3122 6000

Nicholas Brealey Publishing
Hachette Book Group
53 State Street
Boston, MA 02109, USA
Tel: (617) 263 1834

www.nbuspublishing.com

Dedicated to the new Brand You,
the most important
branding challenge of all...
branding yourself

Contents

PART III: GIVING BRAND YOU THE WOW FACTOR

Introduction

Amazingly, my first job was my dream job. Curatorial Assistant in Asian Art at the Seattle Art Museum.

It was the "old" days. Pre-internet. Pre-Zoom. Pre-email. Pre-laptop. Pre-mobile phone. Pre-digital anything. I was hired sight unseen. My job search was conducted entirely through letters sent back and forth. (Today it would be emails, of course, and video interviews.)

I fought for that job, letter by letter. I sent a cover letter and resume to Henry Trubner, the Curator of Asian Art. It was totally a cold call. I couldn't believe it. I got a reply in four days. In his letter Henry mentioned there might be a job since the museum was planning to do a book on its world-renowned Asian art collection.

Hmm...I Had an Idea

I responded immediately. Originally a journalism major before I switched to art history, I pitched myself as "an Asian art historian who can write." In his next letter, arriving five days later, Henry told me there was another candidate he was interested in and wanted to know what salary I was looking for. Shooting off my response letter a day later, I also sent along some writing samples.

Seven days later Henry sent me a job offer. Sometimes you get lucky. Art museums are notoriously difficult to break in to. What lucky timing!

After graduation, I went to my hometown, Miami, Florida, bought a red Volkswagen Beetle, and set off on a leisurely cross-country drive of 3,297 miles to my new job in Seattle. Packed into the car with me was my sister, our camping gear, and all my possessions.

My Terrible-No-Good-Very-Bad First Day

My first day on the job at the Seattle Art Museum is painful to remember and hard to forget. I was confronted by the director of the museum in the office lobby, who told me I didn't have a job!

The curator (Henry, my letter-writing partner) hadn't received permission to hire anyone, the director curtly informed me. I met briefly with Henry, who told me to come back tomorrow and that he would work things out.

Imagine. I was twenty-one years old. I didn't know a soul in Seattle (my sister had flown back to Florida). Rather than landing my dream job, I was caught in the crossfire of these two gentlemen.

The Antidote to Fear Is Action

The worst thing that can happen on your first day on a new job in a faraway city had happened to me. I had moved over three thousand miles, settled into my new apartment, and poof! My dream job was gone.

Back in my car, I started to cry. It was the feeling you have when you realize that your future has turned upside down. I felt like packing my bags and driving away. But where to?

Then I told myself, "Perish the thought." I returned to my apartment and told my landlady (of three days) about my predicament. She asked if I had the letter documenting the job offer. (I did.) "March back in there tomorrow," she said. "That's your contract."

I marched. It worked. My dream job was reinstated.

After that horrible first-day start, Asian art became my life and my brand. I was in deep, working at the museum and then with my PhD studies.

Personal Branding Crisis #1

I began to struggle with the existential questions of my generation "Who am I?" and "Where do I belong?" I began to doubt my career choice. So many thoughts swirled around in my head—"Is this how I should be spending the rest of my life? Life is too short to be in the wrong career."

After my soul searching, I decided to make a dramatic career change and switch back to my original college majors—journalism and advertising. And I knew where I would do it. The capital of the world.

You don't need a connection to New York City to feel its influence, but I did have a connection, and that made the city's gravity a force I could not resist. Heart and head were pulling me.

A Loser Pitch

As you can imagine, with a career change this drastic, it was not easy to get an interview or to find a winning pitch.

Usually interviewers reacted with disbelief when I told them I was trying to transition from being an Asian-art historian to a career in advertising. Then I launched into my pitch: "I'm a hard worker and I want to break into advertising."

Reinventing yourself is as much about
seeing yourself differently
as it is changing how others see you

My elevator pitch was a dud. My positioning was all about me. It was generic. There was no different idea there. There was no benefit, no problem I could solve, except a commitment to work hard.

The result, you guessed it, is that I got rejected again and again. I was traveling through the well-trodden path of rejection.

Radical Reinvention Needed

I found myself branded, but not in the way that I wanted to be branded. I was branded as an academic, as someone too slow and plodding for the ad agency world.

I was getting worried. I couldn't sleep at night. I knew I could do an entry-level advertising job, but how could I convince other people?

Somehow I needed to connect the dots and reinvent myself from an Asian-art historian to an ad person. I drew up a short list of the things I did at the museum that were marketing oriented, such as organizing, promoting, and marketing Asian-art shows.

Eureka! I had the skills. I just needed to frame them better. I had another revelation in doing the experience-listing exercise. A key ability was generating innovative Asian-art exhibit ideas that attracted a wide audience.

I felt a jolt of adrenaline as my ruminations led to my new pitch, a more provocative positioning idea: "I'm a marketer for difficult products."

I compared marketing Asian-art exhibits in a Western culture to marketing a difficult product. It took ingenuity to come up with enticing marketing campaigns and bold, informative Asian-art exhibits that would draw a crowd. I said, "Hire me for one of your tough accounts where you need an innovative problem-solver."

Positioning Brand You in a Sentence

Just like in the branding world, words and phrases count. My new brand positioning—"marketer for difficult products"—got traction.

It was focused. So simple it was easy for interviewers to remember and repeat to others in the interview chain or file away in their minds.

It was different. I never met anyone else who used the "marketer for difficult products" pitch, so it was white space, an open positioning that no one else owned. It enabled me to leapfrog the competition by focusing not on my strength but on how my strength could solve *their* problem.

Finally, my pitch was relevant and memorable. Every ad agency has difficult accounts that few people want to work on. Plus my positioning catchphrase was easy for interviewers to recall and pass along.

A New Identity in the Minds of Others

I was still the same person but I got a totally different response with my new positioning and elevator speech.

And, it was a true story. Your brand narrative always has to be true.

But something important had changed. My new positioning made people see me differently *as if* I was a different person.

I owned a different position in their mind. My positioning turned my perceived negatives (my Asian-art-history job experience and PhD studies) into positives (could handle difficult brand projects).

It was an eye-opening experience, in a good way.

Oversimplify Your Message

You need to craft a cohesive but simple narrative that points people in the direction that you want to take your brand, even if it involves canceling or downplaying something that you are proud of. You must eliminate complexity and confusion so that you have an oversimplified message that gets through.

> You must curate your brand positioning
> by eliminating complexity and confusion

I jettisoned some accomplishments that I was really proud of, like the Asian-art book on the museum's collection I had co-authored and the Japanese art book I had translated. Including these accomplishments destroyed my new personal brand identity and made people brand me as an academic, not a marketer.

Best of all, my new brand positioning got me my first job in advertising, at Trout & Ries Advertising. I learned brand strategy and positioning under the positioning gurus Al Ries (now in the Marketing Hall of Fame) and Jack Trout. Thank you, Al! Thank you, Jack! What a great foundation for beginning in the advertising business.

Tweak Your Pitch

Right from the start, I felt custom built for advertising: the creativity, the analysis, the competitiveness, the hallway brainstorming, the gossip. Then, after I was at the agency for four years, I heard about a job supervising the "I Love New York" campaign at its ad agency, Wells Rich Greene.

It was my new dream job. It was the flagship account at a top creative agency. I'd be part of the team creating high-production-value commercials with celebrities and top Broadway shows. What's not to like?

There were major hurdles, though. Most of my advertising experience was in brand strategy or on business-to-business accounts. The only television experience I had was for a supermarket chain. Not exactly a good match with the job specs.

Research and Discovery

My copywriter friend Bob, who worked at the Wells Rich Greene ad agency, warned me that I didn't have a chance. But he did tell me something valuable, "The account is difficult to manage. Your clients are politicians and career civil servants who rarely agree with each other. The last person didn't stay in the position for long."

Nothing would have changed my mind. Getting this job would be my entre into the big time, on a highly visible creative account. As poorly qualified as I was, I didn't want to lose the opportunity to pitch myself. And my conversation with Bob gave me an idea on how to position myself for the job.

Think Outside In

My first ad boss, Al Ries, always emphasizes that you need to think *"Outside—In."* It's not about what you want to say (Inside), but what your customers want to hear (Outside).

So in the interview, when the hiring manager asked, "Why are you here? You don't have the right background," I was prepared. "My specialty is working on difficult products . . . [*suspenseful pause*] . . . and with difficult clients." I gave examples of building consensus between stakeholders with entrenched, opposing positions in my current job.

His eyes widened. I could see that my pitch was piquing his interest. Maybe I did have a chance.

Now don't misinterpret. I told a true story in my pitch. I did have experience with tough clients.

But I emphasized that skill and customized my interview pitch based on the "research" I had done with Bob. (I didn't share that he had told me that the challenging aspect of the account was working with demanding clients.)

That's how I got hired as Managing Director supervising the "I Love New York" campaign. I got a lot of television experience shooting commercials featuring Broadway shows and celebrities and learned a lot about the big ad agency world.

I loved it! And that's including the challenge of managing a diverse group of strong-willed clients.

Best of all, I learned an important lesson—don't let not being completely qualified for a job stop you!

The Ever-Evolving Personal Brand

When I decided to leave the ad agency world, I set my sights on a corporate advertising job. This time I got branded as an "agency person," someone totally lacking in appeal because I didn't have corporate experience or an MBA. Through a friend, I got an interview with a prominent Wall Street firm.

On the day of the interview, I got stuck in a snow storm in Boston. Even the trains were shut down, so I rented a car and drove to the interview. Given how hard it was to get the interview, I thought to myself, "I'm making this interview, even if I have to walk through snowdrifts."

I spent over ten years on Wall Street as a corporate global brand and advertising executive, through eight mergers and six name changes. That took some personal branding to stay in the game, given the competitive nature of Wall Street businesses. (But that's a whole other book.)

To show you how crazy it was, I started out at Shearson Lehman Brothers when it was a division of American Express and when I left, it was Smith Barney, a division of Citi. And I never changed jobs!

My corporate career ended abruptly on a perfect sunny day, on September 11, 2001.

A Leap to the Wild Side

I'd like to tell you that I became an entrepreneur as a result of careful planning and a blinding flash of insight—a big idea that I knew couldn't fail.

But it didn't happen that way. The truth is, I was forced into entrepreneurship when I lost my high-powered corporate branding job right after 9/11.

Saying goodbye to a Wall Street job—the security, the prestige, the good paycheck—was scary but exciting at the same time. (Never mind that I thought it was my only realistic option.)

Personal branding makes you an
active partner in your career and life destiny

I had periodically harbored thoughts of doing something entrepreneurial at some point (particularly after a bad day at the office). Now, I had to do it. Truth be told, I was burnt out and yearned for more flexibility and control over my career and life. But I struggled with "What should I do next?"

The concept of personal branding was starting to gain traction in the career world around that time. Looking back at my own experience, I realized that building a fulfilling career takes careful, calculated branding at every turn and that led to launching my own company, Selfbrand. Unlike other career coaches and speakers, I was a personal brand strategist applying principles and strategies from the commercial world of brands to the most important brand you'll ever market, Brand You.

Is This Book for You?

The goal of this book is to take you on a personal branding journey, a journey of self-empowerment—that sense of self-awareness and self-fulfillment that brings happiness and is part of life success. Each of us has ideas, abilities, and a unique contribution to make to the world, whether small or large.

Yet many of us shy away from marketing ourselves or making changes, even when we're not happy where we are.

Whether you want to or not, whatever your work circumstances are, you need to think about personal branding today.

You may not have a choice.

You could be a woman working remotely and worried she's been sidelined on the Mommy track. You could be a talented manager who is burnt out and wants more work-life balance and flexibility. You could have quit during the pandemic and want to make a dramatic career change to something more meaningful. You might be a career coach or professor using this book with your clients or students.

Of course, you don't have to believe me about personal branding. You could rely on luck. But most "lucky" people have personal branding to thank for their luck!

Bye-Bye to the Old

We are living in a time of change, a new world of work and living. The pandemic accelerated trends already happening—a more remote, digital and virtual workplace, a less hierarchical organizational structure, and a realignment of industries fueled by new technologies.

Covid also increased the stress and anxiety of the modern workplace and lifestyle. It's not easy to stand out or plan your career moves in a workplace in flux, especially if you're working remotely.

You may not want to get involved in personal branding, but consider this: The world has changed. The well-trodden path from entry level to retirement is long gone. Branding may not be optional anymore. You need to build a brand, not just have a job to succeed in the new world of work. And if you think you are too busy to brand yourself or you dislike reading books cover to cover, this book is designed so that you can read it in chunks.

Here's what's coming up:

Part I Finding the Right Positioning for Brand You in the New World of Work

Quo Vadis?

In the aftermath of the pandemic, many people started thinking about the lives they wanted to have versus the one they were living each day. They started to define their concept of success and how to live their lives. Many wanted more flexibility. Others wanted more control.

The pandemic brought about a quest for meaning in others. A 2021 Pew Research study found that only 17 percent of adults now view their job or career as a source of meaning—down seven percent from four years earlier.[1]

Others discovered during the pandemic that they like the remote nomad lifestyle. They want to remain Zen and don't want to go back to bricks and mortar ever again.

We can all benefit from looking at ourselves through different prisms. The branding world provides a deep reservoir of principles and strategies for finding your vision and your true north.

Positioning Brand You

Your positioning is the foundation of your brand. The book introduces ten of the most successful brand positioning strategies used by big brands that apply to people too. Are you an innovator who's a creative idea person? Are you a leader who inspires people to exceed goals? Or are you a maverick—everything the traditional leader stands for, you stand for the opposite?

You could choose attribute positioning, building your brand on a specific attribute or strength that defines your value added. Or cause positioning, building your brand around a cause that you are devoted to. Or target market positioning, where you focus your brand on a specific audience.

Personal branding makes you an
active partner in your career and life destiny

Each positioning strategy is designed to give you maximum leverage based on your personality, preferences, and abilities, and each chapter provides a template for kickstarting your brand and looking forward to Monday mornings. To help figure out your optimal positioning, you can try my hack, the online Personal Brand Assessment Test in Chapter 3.

Do You Need to Brand?

Personal branding will always be critical as long as talented people have trouble marketing themselves, as long as people want to change careers and "re-brand" themselves for a second act (or third, or fourth), as long as people have to compete through any time of change like the new world of work, as long as people feel marginalized, stuck, or invisible or as long as people want to go out on their own with their own business.

As long as these dynamics exist, people will be looking for ideas and actions that will give them an advantage.

Branding is a great tool because it makes you an active partner in your career and life destiny.

Having desires and goals and then working to accomplish them, is as close as we get to the idea of success, and it's available to everyone, even with our flaws and limitations.

There is no magic wand, but personal branding can be magical. With the right branding, everything can fall into place in terms of how to live and succeed in the new world of work.

PART I:
FINDING THE RIGHT POSITIONING FOR BRAND YOU IN THE NEW WORLD OF WORK

Chapter 1

Know Thyself:
Discovering the New Brand You

One of the earliest insights in the wisdom of civilization is the advice of the Oracle at Delphi, "Know Thyself," inscribed in the seventh century BC above the Temple of Apollo.

The maxim seems simple, so basic. How can I not know myself? Not know what my strengths are or where I belong in the world?

Do you know who you are? Maybe you do. Maybe you don't.

Self-knowledge is not easy. If it was, there wouldn't be so many professional development experts developing online assessment tests to aid in self-discovery. I even created one! (There's a link in Chapter 3.)

Success vs. Happiness

What's the goal of all of this self-discovery? For most, it's about success and happiness, however you define them. If you have both, what more could you want?

To be happy, you must heed the Oracle's advice to "Know Thyself" and create a positive sense of self in your own mind. You must build a sense of self-awareness that blooms into self-actualization, of being who you were meant to be.

But to be successful, you also need to build a positive identity and reputation in the minds of other people. Other people hire you. Or promote you. Or buy from you. Or follow your leadership. Or fire you.

You can't do it alone. You can craft your personal brand, but you don't control it. That power also belongs to other people.

Other people determine your reputation. Other people are also behind your success. Each of us already has a brand in the minds of others, so you might as well make it a strong brand. Especially if you want to compete in today's dynamic anything-can-happen post-pandemic workplace.

That's why you need to learn the currency of personal branding. You need to create a unique brand identity that builds on who you are, your personality and your strengths, and the realities of today's workplace.

Attach an Idea to Yourself

What is branding, really?

Marketers attach an idea to a product, an idea that *positions* the brand with a unique image and identity in the minds of customers.

Personal branding is about attaching an idea to yourself
that's focused, different, and relevant
and gives people a reason to choose you

Likewise, you need to attach a unique positioning idea to yourself in the minds of your "customers"—your boss, colleagues, clients. A positioning that clearly articulates how you are different from competitors.

An Idea That's Focused

You want to attach an idea that positions you in a single sentence. In clear simple language. So simple that anyone can understand, remember, and repeat it. You don't want to be a complicated I-can-do-everything brand.

Rather than going for a "big, complicated" idea, go for a "small, focused" idea. The best positioning ideas are very targeted and specific, not convoluted. Is your positioning idea crisp and clear? Can you write it on the back of a business card? It has to be as simple as that.

An Idea That's Different

You've got to fight the natural instinct to copy the competition. Does your positioning idea set you apart from competitors? Being a me-too brand like "Team player committed to customers" won't get you anywhere. It's so overused and commonplace, the words don't have any meaning anymore.

You'll always be viewed as the generic, so you'd better have a low price.

You know you've found a different idea when you find the *white space,* a need in the marketplace that no one else is filling or no one else can satisfy in quite the way you will.

Of course, be prepared. When you're different, you'll stand out. Personal branding is all about standing out—in a good way—not as a showboater Look at Marie Kondo and her different take on tidiness. Not many people thought much about decluttering their lives, that is until Marie Kondo made organizing your stuff a Zen experience with her trademark phrase "spark joy."

She stood out from other organizers because she emphasized joy not order or control. Her KonMari Method of keeping only what sparks joy and throwing out the rest made her immensely popular. Kondo has appeared on *The Late Show with Stephen Colbert* as well as two Netflix series. A clip of Kondo yelling "I love mess!" became one of *Time* magazine's top ten memes of the year in 2019. Imagine—Kondo became a global brand all because of her fresh take on clutter.

Having a different idea for your brand is powerful. There are many people competing for your job, your opportunity, your ___. It will position you apart from the crowd.

An Idea That's Relevant

Is your brand relevant in today's changing times? What problem or problems do you solve? Think about this. You probably won't get a free ride in the new world of work. You've got to be perceived as bringing value in the current fast-paced business landscape, or you'll be yesterday's news.

Ask yourself, "Where is my industry going?" or "Where is my company going?" or "Will what I do be valuable in the new world of work?" If you're not sure, it's time to get some answers.

An Idea That's Memorable

Finally, it pays to craft your brand positioning idea into an easy-to-remember-and-repeat sentence or catchphrase. You'll be using variations in different settings—job interviews, your online profiles, and networking events.

Nobody pays much attention to dull or wordy narratives. We're living in a time of communication overload, so follow the branding model and make it easy for people to remember you and what you stand for.

Your positioning is your differentiator,
a short phrase that captures
what's special about you and why it matters

Marketers use catch phrases, memorable analogies, and other tricks, and you can too. For example, a financial services executive named Edward, who wanted to get hired in a business role in a dynamic digital company, pitched himself as having the "mind of a businessman and the soul of a creative."

Because he was targeting highly creative companies, Edward emailed a PowerPoint presentation, rather than a traditional resume, to show his creative design and writing skills. It worked. He got a job offer.

Confusion Is Your Enemy

The purpose of positioning is to give you a simple process for establishing a focused brand idea and voice.

The biggest mistake that people make is trying to appeal to everybody. It's like a brand with too many features and too many benefits. A brand that tries to appeal to too many market segments ends up appealing to no one.

It may seem counterintuitive, but you're stronger when you narrow your focus. It's true for products, and it's true for people. You're more effective when you try to appeal to a very specific target audience with a singular idea.

Beware of making a radical about-face in what your brand stands for, like

Ralph Nader did. Nader is an activist well known for his attacks on the establishment, beginning with his 1965 car safety exposé, *Unsafe at Any Speed*, which has sold over a million copies. In 2022, he tried to publish a new book, tentatively titled, *Twelve CEOs I Have Known and Admired*. It was so off-brand, it's been rejected by publishers.[1]

Branding Is About Subtraction

Branding involves letting go. Your brand positioning has to be true and authentic, but you don't have to include everything you've ever done or every strength you have.

Being a Jack or Jill of all trades
is Nowhere's-ville in branding

You must curate your brand and settle on your best positioning idea. You have to be ruthless about how you edit the story you want to tell.

Anything that others could claim just as much as you can, eliminate.

Anything that is complicated, eliminate.

Anything that bogs people down in the past and not the future, eliminate.

Confusion will doom you. And once someone's mind is made up about you, it's almost impossible to change their opinion.

As your focus becomes narrower, something unexpected happens. You eventually become known for your one positioning idea. Your personal brand becomes established.

Better Branding Wins

Sometimes clients tell me they're better than many of their colleagues. They have better credentials, better experience, better whatever. But they're not doing as well as others or didn't get the promotion or didn't get the sale.

It may seem unfair, but being better is often not enough. You need a *different better*. And you need to market your different better.

> The truth is "ability" is often not one of the
> most important attributes for success

The "better" product, by objective standards often doesn't win in the marketplace. The product or person with better branding wins out. You're looking for a different better—*a Unique Selling Proposition (USP)*—a position that no one else has in your competitive set.

Think of your ideal positioning as the conceptual place you want to own in your target customers' minds. You want to stand for something important to your target audience that's different from others. People need to understand how you diverge from standard expectations.

Hard Work + Branding = Success

You might wonder if you should get involved in personal branding, because your hard work should speak for itself. I wish it were so. It rarely does.

Throughout my career, people have told me, "Work hard and you'll be successful." They should have told me, "Work hard and you'll be successful…maybe."

Hard work is important, but it's not enough, even if you show up early every day at company headquarters and your labor is in full sight. If you work remotely from home, much of your hard work is not visible unless you put it on your boss's radar.

Hard Power vs. Soft Power

Success takes two types of power: *hard power* and *soft power*.

Hard power is the tangible, fact-based things you can put on your CV—your experience, degrees, jobs, education, certifications, achievements, and awards.

Of course having the goods is important, just like hard work is important, but it's not enough for success.

The real power today is soft power (or personal branding power)—the invisible, intangible qualities and abilities you can't put on your CV that propel success today.

Soft power is your image and reputation. Your communications ability and verbal identity. Your network and partnerships. Your executive presence and visual identity. It's your visibility in your company, community, or industry. Your ability to connect with others. Your trustworthiness. Even your personality, and especially your likability.

Personal branding power means:

Having a *purpose,* your *why* you do what you do

Having a *positioning,* your *what* you do differently than others

Having an *action plan,* your *how* you bring value and accomplish goals

---

Begin with Free Association

Before we get into a formal analysis of the best positioning for Brand You, do this exercise.

Take out a blank piece of paper. Write down your name. Then write down whatever first comes to mind as your brand positioning statement.

The idea is to capture free thinking before your mind is contaminated by research, facts, and group think. Your gut and intuition may have powerful ideas on how to brand yourself.

You can do a version of the exercise by yourself or with a few other people to create an *ideation tree* or *mind map*. It's a great way to explore different ideas and options in a visual format. The best ideas and strategies often come through brainstorming with the type of free association you do with others who have different backgrounds.

Early in my career, I was trying to break into advertising after a career as an art historian specializing in Asian art. Brainstorming with a friend led to a breakthrough idea, positioning myself as a "marketer for difficult products" since it took creativity to come up with innovative Asian art exhibits that attracted a wide audience in the United States.

It's All About Perceptions

When people see you, what thoughts pop into their minds? That is what branding is really about. The reality is that your brand is what other people say about you when you're not around.

When it comes to branding,
perception is more important than reality

If people think you are management material, you will be. If senior leaders think you are mediocre, you won't be on the fast track until you change their perceptions. If people don't even think about you at all because you're invisible working remotely, you've got a perception problem too. Following branding principles and strategies can help you create positive, meaningful perceptions about Brand You.

How can you find out what others think about you? Listen. What do others compliment you on? What do they criticize you about? Ask for feedback after you make a presentation. If you work at a corporation, your annual review will tell you a lot about what your boss thinks about Brand You.

Think Outside In: Customer First

To brand yourself well, you have to begin with your target audience (Outside). You need to understand their problems and needs. You need to step inside their shoes before you figure out what you want to say (Inside).

Brand experts often put together a *customer persona*, a detailed description or visualization of an "ideal customer." Your "customers" are everyone you need to influence to achieve your goals. So if you're in a company, your "customers" could include your boss, senior managers, and team members. If you are an entrepreneur, it's the customers for your products and services.

Try to imagine your typical customer as a specific person: How do they look? What's their lifestyle? What makes them tick? What are they worried about?

What benefits do you bring that they want? Do you connect with them emotionally? Drill down. What vexes them? What challenges do they face? How do they like to consume information? Even if your target audience is a group of colleagues at your company, you should find this exercise immensely helpful.

What is your target audience looking for?
How can you be that person?

Go to School on Your Competition

If you need to compete in a crowded, competitive marketplace, you need to know who your competition is. We all have competitors (though you might not like to refer to them that way).

It's a fact. A competitor is anyone who is pursuing the same goal or target market that you are pursuing.

That's why it's important to understand your competition and what they stand for, and how you are not them. Analyze them in a short *competitive analysis*. Know what your key competitors' strengths are and, most importantly, be able to define their weaknesses. Ideally, you want to position your strengths against their weaknesses and reposition their strengths as less important attributes.

Your goal is to be perceived as clearly different from competitors in an important way. Try to frame your differentiator in a sentence. Fill in the blank:

Unlike others who do what I do, I _____.

Brand Audit: The SWOT Analysis

Marketers often use a handy analysis called the SWOT analysis, a snapshot look at a brand's strengths, weaknesses, opportunities, and threats.

The SWOT analysis can be a useful tool for you too, especially in today's fast-changing world of work. It is an intensive look at your strengths and weaknesses in a real-world framework. It will help you focus on your strengths and deflect your weaknesses. It will help you zero in on opportunities and threats on your professional horizon.

For example, in my own SWOT analysis done during the pandemic, I realized that in the current world of work, many people would need personal branding skills in order to stand out and succeed. The move to remote and hybrid settings and technology-driven changes made personal branding more important than ever. The new world of work wasn't a threat for me personally, but an opportunity.

Doing a periodic SWOT analysis will keep you on track, especially in today's dynamic world.

Personal Brand Audit: The SWOT Analysis

1. Strengths: Write down anything that you are good at and love to do. Write down what your boss, clients, or colleagues give you high marks on. Include skills, abilities, and personality traits that contribute to your success.

2. Weaknesses: Write down what you're terrible at and hate to do, or areas where your boss and friends criticize you.

3. Opportunities: This is wide open. Write down anything that could be an opportunity for you. A key is to look for unmet or new needs brought about by the new world of work.

4. Threats: What's changing in your industry that keeps you awake at night about yourself, your career, business, or the economic outlook.

How-To and How-to-Think

To create a personal brand, you need to create a clear identity of who you are not only in your own mind, but in the minds of others.

You're looking for a positioning that is authentic. (Contrary to what you might think, good branding always has to be true.) You need a positioning that is different from others and gives people a reason to choose you. Being a generic, one-of-many brand won't cut it, nor will a brand that's mired in the past.

In the personal branding mindset, you are your most important asset—an asset like education and career achievements that no one can take away from you. Personal branding shows you how to increase the value of that asset, both in terms of self-actualization—becoming who you can be—and in terms of maximizing your career success.

> Personal branding is always about authenticity,
> but it means showing yourself in the most appealing way

The best place to start in defining your brand is simply to begin with the truth. Who you are and can be. Personal branding is also about self-empowerment. You must take control of your career narrative and career destiny especially today. No one can do it for you.

A Brand For All Seasons

There will be strong economies when jobs are plentiful and weak markets when the job market is dismal. There will be one constant, though: You will need personal branding to be in charge in the new world of work, a world scarred by a pandemic, buoyed by technology, and undergoing rapid change.

You have to stand out and stand for something of value. You need a positioning that meets a need in the marketplace and clearly differentiates you from others.

We're all on camera now. We all need to be producers of our brand narrative.

As a personal brander, you must always be relevant, find new opportunities, and stay on top of how you are perceived by your target markets.

We spend too much of our time following rules or simply plodding ahead. We don't see an opportunity or how the world is changing in ways that affects our livelihood. Make some time to ruminate about what's happening and how it affects you.

Then take charge of your brand. Commit to taking an active rather than a passive role in defining yourself and your future.

Chapter 2

Personal Branding May No Longer Be Optional

There once was a time when you dressed up and went to the office every day. When you mainly met with your work colleagues in person. When your biggest job worry was your commute. When you even thought of where you wanted your career to be in five years.

That was yesterday.

Now we're living in a time of change and uncertainty, a new digitally driven work landscape that's been altered by a pandemic. Innovative new technologies, along with the maturing of the internet, have initiated the biggest transformation in how business is conducted that we've ever experienced. And the rate of technological change is not expected to decline. Business prognosticators predict that we're likely to see new types of job specs and the demise of familiar ones in our future.[1]

How will this tsunami of change affect the way we live and work in the future? Do you have any idea? Nobody does. The only consensus, though, without any doubt, is that we won't be returning to business as usual.

Surprise Success—Remote Working

While in the beginning of the Covid-19 pandemic not everyone took the pandemic seriously, many businesses were quick to innovate and adapt.

Productivity didn't suffer except for industries like manufacturing and hospitality, where remote work was difficult or impossible for most employees to do.

In many ways the pandemic was a victory for workers. Workers loved their newly found freedom. Goodbye to the long commute and dressing up. Hello to comfortable, casual clothes and working when and where you want.

Most businesses carried on with few hiccups or losses in productivity. In one study of remote workers, 40 percent said they were more efficient, 45 percent said they were about equally efficient, and only 15 percent said they were less efficient than when they worked in the office.[2]

Many were shocked at how well remote working worked. The 2021 World Happiness Report showed that even with the global hardship from the pandemic, life satisfaction remained steady in 2020, from the previous year.[3]

Big Surprise: The Great Resignation

Another outcome of the pandemic was how many people dropped out of the workforce. It was definitely an unexpected development.

Most labor laws favor employers, and for the last four decades, the leverage over jobs and wages was clearly on the side of management.

Then, during the pandemic economy, the pendulum swung swiftly toward employees. The tightness of the labor market gave employees leverage, power, and options.[4]

Companies started listening to their employees because the demand for talent was greater than the supply. Nevertheless, many employees opted out of the labor market to figure out what they wanted to do next knowing that jobs were plentiful.

Others used the time in lockdown to create a new business. New-business formation increased over 40 percent in 2020.[5] Many hopped on an exciting new trend—tiny microbusinesses—built around themselves and an area of expertise.[6]

Power to the People

White-collar employees got used to logging on from their bedroom home offices during the pandemic and liked the flexibility of working remotely. Some didn't want to go back to the office full-time or even part-time.

There was a rise in employee activism, with workers advocating for more pay, increased flexibility, reduced hours, and more time off. Many companies changed their policies in response to worker demands. Large companies realized that they needed multiple work options. Ceding more control to employees is a dramatic change from the past.

The pandemic fueled a reevaluation of our lives. An Ipsos study in October 2021 reported that 54 percent of Americans are rethinking their life priorities and prioritizing a better work-life balance with 20 percent saying these changes were driven by the pandemic.[7]

The Great Reset

A great reset about work is taking place, and work is not likely to go back to its pre-pandemic ways. We're in a new, more technology-driven work world that gives us many options for how work life can be structured.

And it's about time. The modern company structure, created after World War II on a military model with a strict hierarchy, is not as relevant today. While the hierarchical paradigm can lead to amazing productivity, it can stifle innovation, slow down decision making and be difficult environment for creating a company culture.

Many companies are examining their workplace beginning with who can work from home and who can't. Most of those who can are knowledge workers, who make up over half of workers. The challenge is how to multiply decision-making so that the modern organization is successful, efficient and culturally rich.

Those who can't work from home are mainly in manufacturing, retail, hospitality and healthcare. This group wants a reset too: in better working conditions, pay, and benefits.

More Flexibility, Please

Work is being redesigned. It may not be a physical place anymore. Work is what you do.

Workers started speaking up during the pandemic and they told us loud and clear what they wanted—flexibility. The success of remote working proved that other ideas for workplaces can be effective and *where* you work wasn't as critical as most business leaders assumed.

Ninety-five percent of people wanted flexible hours, compared with 78 percent who wanted location flexibility, in a November 2021, Global Pulse survey of 10,000 knowledge workers sponsored by Future Forum.[8]

> People want flexibility,
> not a one-size-fits-all work world

It's not necessarily a one-option situation, either. Employees want the freedom to choose. Should the workplace be hybrid, remote, or completely in office? Should it be the same system for all? Or work from anywhere? Or in-office but with more flexibility than in the past?

Hybrid a Win-Win?

The hybrid office could be the solution. The default for the majority of companies is a best-of-both-worlds scenario: a hybrid office with three days in the office when a lot of meetings and socializing can take place, and two days WFH where solitary work can get done.[9]

Employees get flexibility working remotely, and the company preserves the one-to-one interaction so important to innovation, decision making, and culture.

Other companies want everyone back in the office, and many employees are okay with that if there is more flexibility in work schedules.

Some companies, particularly in tech, are choosing the boundary-free route, going 100 percent remote. Having no boundaries means you can work with the best and the brightest no matter where in the world you live, without having to relocate.

And that sounds great.

Still to be solved, though, is how do you feel that you belong—a sense of community and culture—in a totally remote company? Plus there are other complications.

More Risk of Invisibility

Working remotely has many advantages, particularly if you have a long commute or want to run a load of laundry while you attend a meeting. But relationship building and visibility are not among them. And that can put you at a disadvantage.

Some say the concept of face time is overrated, but I think the reality is that avoiding face-to-face, real-time personal contact can lead to your demise in the workplace. You've got to make sure you're an important part of the team, and visibility with real-time contact is an important part of that.

Is face time overrated and unnecessary?
I say, "Avoid it at your peril!"

The way to succeed is by being known and remembered. How do you advance yourself or get rewarded for great performance when your company can't see you working remotely? How do you attract bigger possibilities unless people know you well in person and virtually?

It's easy to be invisible in a traditional workplace, and your lack of visibility is compounded in the remote or hybrid world. It's easier to be invisible and forgotten.

FOMO or Just MO?

People who work together in a traditional office have a much richer personal experience and exposure to senior executives and coworkers. Face-to-face interaction is critical for culture and innovation, many managers believe.

If you decide to WFH and just occasionally or almost never drop into the office, you've got to worry about FOMO (fear of missing out).

For many it will simply be MO.

What You Can Miss

You may miss out on the quick, impromptu meetings in the hall with senior leaders and colleagues that bloom into a thirty-minute conversation.

The "Do you have a minute to discuss a new project?" or "Hmm...I didn't know you had experience in that area" encounters that can lead to a new opportunities and promotions.

As every manager knows,
the easiest people to promote are the ones you know;
and the hardest people to let go are the ones you know

Being known and recognized is important. Being unknown is a career dead end.

Belonging in a Virtual World

Creating relationships and community is important for a company's success and for yours, too. If you're working remotely or in a hybrid setup, you need to align with a company that is creating intentional opportunities and structures for community, socializing, and mentorship. Or you can feel isolated, like an outsider, or caught up in a transactional work environment.

There's all those cultural moments and opportunities you could miss out on. How do you build a reputation or onboard virtually at a new job? Or learn the company culture when you are working remotely? Or bond with mentors? Or get access to the same learning as in-person employees?

Get on the Radar

If you're remote, you can't just knock on a senior manager's door and say, "Let's chat." And you'll be competing with ambitious coworkers who maximize their office time to their advantage and show up when the boss is in.

You can lose out on so many of the relationship-building encounters and ad hoc meetings that used to be part of everyday life when you were in the office full-time. Like asking colleagues personal questions about how their kids are doing, which isn't likely to be brought up on a virtual call. Or the opportunity to meet senior members of different teams, or just bump into people in the hall.

Imagine. An impromptu meeting happens between your boss and your team. You'll be out of the loop unless you're called in virtually. But let's get real: How many times will people take the time to do that?

Decisions will have to be made without you. Working remotely, you could often be playing catch-up or, even worse, being ghosted. What do you do if you're left off team emails and Slack messages? Of course, it can be an accidental oversight, but by the time you find out, you're behind on project deadlines.

You may even feel very productive at home but you need to actively set up fifteen-minute coffee chats with your boss and other senior managers each week so they know what you're up to. Use these micromoments to share what you're working on and ask about side projects you could help with.

Does Remote = Less Than?

The remote workplace may have other drawbacks. In a Microsoft study of over 60,000 remote employees, cross-team collaboration was more static and siloed.[10]

According to productivity experts, cross-group collaboration and strong ties are the keys to unlocking creativity. But in the Microsoft study, there was one stunning communication trend among those working remotely: Individual teams got closer. Those cohorts soared.

It was the bonding effect of being in a pod.

Unfortunately, opting for remote work can send the wrong message to some senior managers. Tech firms, including Twitter, Shopify, and Drop-Box, jumped on the remote bandwagon, but some business titans question the home-based employee's work ethic. JP Morgan CEO, Jamie Dimon, famously declared that remote work "doesn't work for those who want to hustle."[11] (By the way, there is no evidence that remote workers are slackers; in fact quite the contrary.)

A Two-Class System?

Some workplace experts fear that in-person, hybrid, and remote workplaces will result in a two-tiered work environment. They forecast that on-site employees will get the recognition and promotions and remote workers will lag behind as second-class citizens or orphans.[12]

The remote worker penalty:
the perception that you're not a "real" member of the team

In short, you're penalized if you're not physically present. It's the In-Office Folks versus the Remotes, which will likely end up as the Haves versus the Have-Nots based on your proximity to your company's power center.

The reality is, no matter how many check-ins you set up with your boss on your calendars, you can't keep in touch and connect with your boss like you did when you sat one desk over.

Working remotely can put you at a disadvantage compared to colleagues who do sit one desk over from the boss. There's value in being able to look someone in the eye in their office versus scheduling a video call.

The two-class system is expected to hurt women more than men. One survey, by LinkedIn, showed women were 25 percent more likely to request working remotely.[13]

Offsite as the New On-site

To establish a sense of culture, connection, and mission among disparate groups, some companies are looking at innovative models, like using "offsite as the new on-site."[14] They're setting up short off-site gatherings at hotels, Airbnb mansions, spas—even outdoors or in the office—as a way for everyone to meet in person. The idea is to keep the freedom of remote work but bring back the social connection and creative brainstorming from the old office days.

Setting up off-sites can be a logistical nightmare. Companies are looking for technology to help plan the meetings so they are cost effective and there's a balance of socializing, reconnecting, building trust, and getting work done.

Still to be determined is how often these off-site meetings should take place—monthly, every six weeks, quarterly—to ensure that culture and connection occur whether you are a remote, hybrid, or in-office worker.

Our Overcommunicated World

Our attention span is down to a few seconds. We were already on the road to communication burnout before the pandemic. Now it's even worse, no doubt about that.

Just ask the people wading through a deluge of online communications and meeting requests every day, all made possible by technology and the move to more matrixed, de-layered organizations. That means more bosses and teams to be kept in the loop and more meetings to attend.

It used to take a seasoned audio-visual expert and big fancy equipment to set up a video conference. Now, with Zoom and Microsoft Teams, anyone, even a child, can do it.

Then there's the relentless march of emails, texts, and messaging apps on your smartphone and laptop. The internet makes it easy to connect every hour, wherever you are (and some bosses think you should be available practically every hour).

Surprisingly, technology may not have decreased your workload. Many of us are more swamped than ever.

Living at Work

We thought technology was supposed to shrink work time, but it hasn't worked out that way. As one employee said, it's not "working at home;" it's "living at work."

A Harvard Business School study in 2020 looked at the email and calendar data of over three million workers at 2,900 companies, in 16 global cities.[15] The average daily workload increased by 48 minutes, and the number of meetings increased by 13 percent after the Covid lockdown started. The average workday increased over a whopping 8 percent.

Welcome to the 100-hour workweek.

In an attempt at better work-life balance, some employers are setting limits with "core hours" when employees have to be "on." Many employees are lobbying for better work-life balance with enforced off-limits times such as evenings and weekends.

Rise of the Contingent Class

Gig work might be in your future, if it isn't already. Forty percent of the US workforce is made up of contingency workers according to the US Government Accountability report.[16] Companies are expected to expand their use of freelance workers to 50 percent of the US workforce by 2050.

The increasing usage of freelance talent is not just a US phenomenon, either. According to an Oxford Economics survey, over 80 percent of executives in 27 countries plan to increase their contingent employees.[17]

While it can come with more freedom, and that's very appealing, being classified as a contingent worker has its cons. Just talk to the growing numbers of gig workers, freelancers, and independent contractors about the lack of benefits and job security.

If you go the contingent worker route, by choice or by edict, you must master personal branding so you stand for something of value and have options. Contingent workers are often the first to go when there's an economic downturn.

Your Sell-By Date

You also have to brand yourself as a defense against irrelevance due to the fast pace of change and technologies like AR (augmented reality), automation, and other innovations that are affecting us. Technology has made the world more automated and eliminated many boring and repetitive tasks, but it's also made the workplace more competitive, fast-paced, and global.

Technology futurists predict that mobile, wearable, and embedded computing will further change how and where people gather and share information.

Who's Looking Out for You?

You have to keep on your toes in the new world of work for other reasons, too.

Big Brother may be watching. There's more monitoring of how you spend your day such as virtual clock in and out, tracking work computer usage and monitoring emails and other internal communications through surveillance software.

So watch out if you are using devices provided by your company. Best to have personal conversations and activities on your own devices.

The metamorphosis of the workplace can make anyone feel uneasy. We have to accept that change is no longer unusual, it's the rule.

Transformation is the new status quo. You can't rely on the company to take care of you. That went away with the gold watch upon retirement. Most companies are fighting for their own survival anyway.

You have to take care of yourself.

The New Metaverse of Work

Companies are exploring AR and other technologies to create a *metaverse* for highly realistic interactive meetings and encounters. Everyone, or at least their avatars, will seem to be in the same room even when they are thousands of miles apart.

The pandemic and rise of new technologies sped up the convergence already taking place in the worlds of virtual, gaming, real life, and social media. Who knows if and how the metaverse and physical worlds will continue to converge.

In October 2021, at the unveiling of the rebranding of Facebook as Meta, we got an introduction to what the metaverse might look like. Mark

Zuckerberg (known in the metaverse as Mark Z) gave us a virtual tour of the upcoming immersive world for work and play. It's a world where there are no boundaries. You can make your avatar be and look like anything you want.

Branding Nirvana or Chaos?

So where does that leave you as a personal brander? Will the plethora of options be personal branding heaven or total confusion?

From a branding perspective, you want everything to be on brand. There needs to be a narrative thread that connects the IRL (in real life) person and your avatar.

It's hard enough to be recognized for one thing, and a total mess if you have multiple personalities and incarnations on the metaverse, in person and online.

What's Your Future?

All the advantages of the new world of work is countered by its challenges. The pandemic got a lot of people thinking about what they didn't like about their work life. And the angst wasn't just a U.S. phenomenon. More than three quarters of Britons said they were thinking of making big changes in their work life according to think tank Global Future.[18]

There is a tremendous desire for more flexibility in how we work and how we live. But you'll also need flexibility in how you envision your career to be able to navigate through changing economies and new technologies. Many of us may need to switch jobs to stay relevant in a fast-changing world. Best to align yourself with a company that fosters community and has programs in place to help you succeed in the new world of work.

Whatever your path, personal branding can help you stay in control of your career on your own terms.

The world has changed. Are you ready for it?

Chapter 3

Ten Timeless Strategies and Seven New Realities in the New World of Work

F inding the right positioning is everything. The Top Ten Positioning Strategies contain wisdom that is timeless and true, and they are used by big brands today. And they work for Brand You, too.

In positioning strategy, it's not so much about building your brand but *becoming* your brand. It's about uncovering your unique value. The following chapters will help you do the analysis required to become the person you want to present to the world. There is no shortcut.

We will cover each distinct positioning in a separate chapter. You can examine the personality and social and psychological profile of each positioning. You'll read about examples from the branding world, well-known personalities, and everyday employees and professionals. (Which one or two sound like you?)

Each chapter ends with exercises for summarizing your positioning into a crisp *personal brand statement*—your brand in a sentence—that communicates what's different about you, identifying your *keywords* and key support points. So it will be easy for you to put together your bio and brand narrative.

Your Positioning Is Your Guide

Your positioning strategy is your guide to your personal brand development. It's your road map to follow in marketing yourself.

Your positioning sets up everything: Your value proposition, brand personality, elevator pitch, visual identity, verbal identity, and marketing activities. Your positioning makes it easy to determine if something is on brand or off brand.

The Top 10 Positioning Strategies

1. Innovator
2. Leader
3. Maverick
4. Attribute
5. Engineer
6. Expert
7. User
8. Elite
9. Heritage
10. Cause

The only popular positioning strategy I didn't include is *Low Price*. I figured that if you're reading this book, you didn't want to compete at a bargain price.

Try My Hack: The Online Personal Brand Finder: http://selfbrand.com/personalbrandfinder.html

My online assessment test is designed to help you find your positioning advantage.

The algorithm behind it increases the odds you'll get the "right" answer—the best positioning based on your psychological type.

There's nothing to stop you from choosing a brand strategy that you feel offers you the best leverage based on your strengths and preferences and building up expertise in that area.

Trust your gut. It's often smarter than your brain. I've done it. You can too.

Make Mistakes

Finding the best positioning strategy is not easy for you, for me, or for other top marketers. You might not get your positioning right the first time, but don't let that stop you. Even big brands can struggle to find the right positioning.

When Volvo was first being launched in the United States in the 1950s and 1960s, it explored different positioning strategies.[1]

In the 1950s, Volvo positioned its pricey car as a "second vehicle" for owners. With its high sticker price, many Americans couldn't afford a Volvo as a second car, so the marketing campaign fell flat. Volvo car sales in the US were low.

In 1959, Volvo switched ad agencies and went with a campaign around the attribute "quality" (using Attribute Positioning Strategy No. 4), but sales were still disappointing.

Shifting ad agencies again, Volvo selected a different attribute, "durability," taking aim at the quick obsolescence of American cars at the time.

Does Your Positioning Click?

None of Volvo's positioning strategies resonated with American consumers. It wasn't until 1970, when Volvo settled on a different attribute (and yet another ad agency), that things changed for the Swedish car maker.

"Safety" was a new and different attribute, a positioning not used by other cars up to that time. The safe-car positioning clicked with American consumers and Volvo became a big player in the American car market. Now, of course, other car brands are catching up with Volvo's safety vision.

New Reality No. 1: Assess Whether Your Career Path Is On Trend

There are also new realities you have to contend with in the new world of work.

Futurists predict continuous, dynamic change in the workforce—the rise of new "work" and the demise of traditional ones. They predict many of us will be changing jobs multiple times, either by choice or necessity, in the new world of work.[2]

You know you have a problem if a robot could potentially do your job (or parts of your job). Then you know you need radical reinvention.

But what do you do if your industry is changing and your area of expertise isn't as valued as it once was? The first thing you need to do is assess where you are now. Ask yourself, "What is the future for what I do? Do I need new skills?"

The future was precisely Erin's worry. Erin was scared of going in the direction of the dinosaurs, since she was a traditional marketer in a digital world.

If you're not included in key meetings,
it's time to send out SOS signals

Erin had a reason to be worried. Her boss's role as Chief Marketing Officer was eliminated, and everyone in the marketing department now reported to the Chief Digital Officer.

Like in many companies, digital marketing was overtaking traditional marketing.

Erin had little experience in social media or in digital analytics. She realized that she wasn't an asset in marketing meetings like she had been before. Now digital and social media campaigns were getting all the attention and the biggest share of the budget.

New Reality No. 2: Imagine Your Best Future

Erin suddenly realized that she could be out of the game and might be approaching the end of her career. And she was only in her late thirties!

She needed a major brand overhaul. She built her digital credentials, the new land of opportunity, by taking courses and attending digital conferences.

Erin repositioned herself as No. 6 Expert. She positioned herself as a rare combo, a digital marketing expert with a strong background in traditional marketing. Her new positioning and credentials led to a digital marketing role that offered a better future.

New Reality No. 3: Launch a Personal Marketing Plan

In the new world of work, visibility is more important than ever. You can't hide under a rock, if you want to advance.

That's why if your company has gone hybrid, the smart choice is to mimic your boss's schedule so that you have lots of face-time opportunities. But maybe that's not what you want to do.

The big mistake people make is assuming good work will get noticed on its own. It wasn't true pre-pandemic, and it's not true now. (Unless you are lucky, very lucky.) When you're working remotely from home, you are visibility challenged. And that can hurt you, as Josh discovered.

Don't assume your work will speak for itself.
It's your job to get your work in front of the right people.

His workstyle has always been to work on his own, with little supervision. It worked well in the past when he could easily have spontaneous encounters with his boss and do a quick check-in after a meeting.

Josh's workstyle even worked well when everyone was remote during the pandemic. Post-pandemic, Josh chose to abandon his long commute and work remotely full-time, while his boss and most coworkers chose hybrid or on-site working.

Now Josh's quiet nose-to-the-grindstone-text-only workstyle is a liability.

His boss started asking questions like "How long did this project take?" and "How many hours did you work yesterday?" Wow. That's not the type of questions you want to hear from your boss.

Whether he wanted to or not, Josh needed to get out of the shadows. Toiling away out of sight remotely with the occasional text wasn't working. Josh needed to change his boss's perceptions.

New Reality No. 4: Ramp Up Real-Time Contact

The obvious fix was for Josh to communicate more, but how? There are two basic modes of communication that disparate teams can use:

- **Real-time synchronous communication** is when messages are shared in real time, like phone calls and face-to-face and video meetings.
- **Asynchronous communication** is when messages are sent and consumed without regard to time and place, like emails, texts, and online forums.[3]

The default channel for many remote workers like Josh is asynchronous communication, like email, because it's so efficient. Plus, you can avoid the hassle of real-time communication and potential awkwardness and pesky questions.

Beware! You need to bring context to your work and have back-and-forth dialogue with your boss and senior managers, and that can only be done easily with synchronous communication. Otherwise, you can end up isolated from your boss and peers. And that is never good.

There's nuance and connection in real-time conversations
that isn't likely to occur in emails and texts

If you're not going to be in the office, you need a daily and weekly communication plan that works for your boss and you. If you want to advance in your career, though, a non-real-time, asynchronous communication style is not good enough.

You need to step out of your comfort zone and mix it up with real-time contact too, whether it's in-person or Zoom or even the phone. If your company is having on-site or off-site meetings, take advantage of the opportunity to socialize, meet new people, and collaborate. Many companies offer virtual mentoring programs with senior managers that you can set up.

Without a communication plan with key players at your company, you miss out on the deep relationships that are more likely to form in real-time conversations. And that can end up hurting your career prospects.

New Reality No. 5: Articulate Your Value

Humility may be a virtue in some realms, but not so much in the business world.

Based on his findings from the Personal Brand Finder online tool, Josh built his brand using Strategy No. 5 Engineer. In evaluating his strengths, he realized that he was the programmer who solved difficult programming problems through sheer persistence. He positioned himself as the "patient, persistent tinkerer who solves tough programming problems." It resonated with his boss and team members because it was true.

It's your job to communicate your value,
not your boss's job to figure it out

Josh shared short recaps of his solutions with his boss on one-to-one video calls backed up with an emailed status report. He set up a personal website and LinkedIn profile to have more visibility in the wider world. He also made more of an effort to be part of the company culture on virtual happy hours and other company events.

Maybe Josh's work should have spoken for itself. Maybe he shouldn't be penalized if he didn't like to promote himself and tended to avoid real-time encounters. But now his boss could clearly see what Josh was up to and see how he was a valuable member of the team.

New Reality No. 6: Seek Strong Partnerships

Brand managers spend a lot of time selecting an ad agency, digital partners, and marketing strategists. Likewise, you need to take a hard look at your alliances.

With the rise of remote and hybrid workplaces, you have more flexibility on where you work. Make sure you have a strong Brand You team.

- **Company:** No matter how talented you are, it's a bad move to cast your fate with a clunker company. Are you working at a company making yesterday's products and services or that's going somewhere? Is the culture right for your values and work preferences? Do they provide opportunities to socialize and collaborate at off-site meetings if you're a remote worker? If so, let them know you are on their team. If not, finding a new company has to be in your marketing plan.
- **Boss:** You always want to work for the best and the brightest. Is your boss smart and plugged in with the senior leaders at your company? Does he surprise you with, "Hey, great project! Why don't you take the day off tomorrow" emails? Is she sponsoring you for advancement? Or recommending you for high-visibility assignments? If you're not on the fast track, it's time to send up SOS signals. You aren't going anywhere until you get a different boss.
- **Business colleagues:** You need business friends of all types, both inside and outside your company, not just personal friends. Why? For referrals. (You'll find you get most jobs through business friends, often ones that you don't know well.) Ask for feedback. (You need smart people for brainstorming your positioning, marketing, and social media tactics.) This is a group you always need to be expanding.

New Reality No. 7: Accept Change as the New World of Work

The metamorphosis of the workplace can make anyone feel uneasy. We have to accept that change is probably not that unusual anymore. It's the norm.

We've all mastered having a virtual business meeting, doctor's appointment, company happy hour, or family gathering without going anywhere.

But there still can be a lack of real human connection in remote working and virtual meetings unless your company has frequent off-site or on-site gatherings for in-person interaction.

New developments in AR, VR, and other technologies are creating new virtual realities—metaverses—that bring digital objects into our real world, like holograms. Coworkers in meetings will look like they are there with you, or at least their avatars will be. It will be a big change from being stuck in a box on a Zoom screen, but will we want to work in the metaverse?

To be determined. And who knows what else is coming down the pike.

The New Brand You

If you're forearmed, you'll be able to deal with the changing workplace. Personal branding was always important to stand out and succeed, but it's even more relevant in today's age of transformation.

We're not in Kansas anymore, Toto
It's a new world of work

Sometimes you get lucky and you're working a tight economy where employees have more leverage and jobs are plentiful, like what occurred after the pandemic. Or you're in a career where you're in demand and you don't have a lot of competitors. But you can't rely on everything falling your way all the time.

There's never been a time when it's more important to understand how to brand yourself for success. Having a positioning strategy and game plan gives you a lot of advantages. It forces you to stand out with a distinct positioning idea and to have a game plan—specific actions you are going to do to achieve your goals.

If you always do the same thing, you will only achieve what you have now, or you could even lose ground in today's dynamic workplace.

Personal branding forces you to think about yourself, your career strategy, and how you want to live. That's an advantage over most people, and it's especially important in the new world of work.

PART II:
INTRODUCING THE TOP 10 PERSONAL BRAND POSITIONING STRATEGIES

Chapter 4

Positioning Strategy No. 1 Innovator

Innovators are forward thinking and attracted to the thrilling creativity of innovation. They imagine. They open our eyes to possibilities. They change our perceptions. They challenge us to think in new ways.

They don't ask for permission or forgiveness. Innovators are risk takers who forge ahead with their inventions.

As an innovator, you must have great confidence in your own creativity, intelligence, and vision. You can be counted on to come up with an innovative solution to a perplexing problem. You strive to be the first to create something revolutionary, and your breakthroughs are the core of your personal brand identity.

You like to brainstorm with others to come up with novel ideas. You are an early adopter of new trends. You're not afraid to step into uncharted territory. In fact, it invigorates you. Being an innovator puts you on the cutting edge of what's new and positions you as a driving force in your company.

Of course, when you are presenting ideas that are new and startling, you're likely to hear "You're planning to do *what*?" or "That's impossible." But as an innovator, you are good at deflecting the concerns of those who don't get your ideas and solutions.

Are You an Innovator?

Do you see yourself as an idea person? A creative problem solver?

Do you see how things can be improved and like to "fix" things?

Do you like to brainstorm with creative people to come up with innovative ideas?

Do you see unique opportunities for innovation in a crisis or time of change?

Do you have confidence in your creativity, intelligence, and vision?

Are you actively looking for a big idea?

If you answered yes to many of these questions, then you may want to position yourself using Positioning Strategy No. 1 Innovator.

Innovator Positioning: I am an innovator because _____

The Innovator Personality

You are a creative, open-minded thinker who isn't afraid of taking risks.

You are often the first person to come up with new options and fresh ideas. People see you as forward thinking, even visionary.

Your discoveries and innovative, creative abilities are not surprising, given your interest in new technologies, processes, techniques, and product ideas. You have a knack for integrating diverse information and redefining problems to generate ideas that deviate from the norm.

In fact, the more complicated a problem is, the more excited you get.

Unlike many people, you handle ambiguity well. You thrive in entrepreneurial environments where creativity and freedom are encouraged, and your different, even quirky, personality and lifestyle are accepted.

You're bold and you excite others with your passion and enthusiasm. As a risk taker, you like to take on a challenge and see it through to success. You like working in companies where you have time for creative ideas to ferment. In meetings, you're likely to be the first to ask "Why not?" and "What about…" You like to explore the possibilities.

Your colleagues often see you as an independent spirit but can get frustrated when you're impulsive and change direction quickly. But that's why you're a creative genius.

Most of the time you:	*But sometimes you:*
■ Are a risk taker	■ Want things to fit your vision
■ Come up with many solutions	■ Think your solution is best
■ Are on top of new trends	■ Are impulsive and prone to changing direction

Generally people see you as:	*But you can:*
■ Highly creative and aesthetic	■ Ignore creativity of others
■ Open-minded and curious	■ Be intolerant of pedestrian ideas
■ Brimming with ideas and new projects	■ Be arrogant

If this sounds like you, all the more reason to explore positioning yourself using Positioning Strategy No. 1 Innovator.

The First Mover Advantage

Getting into the mind of consumers first with a new idea or revolutionary product gives you an enormous advantage, the *first mover advantage.*

Very often, the first brand to innovate or to be recognized as the innovator ends up as the most well known and the leader in the category. Think Phil Knight and Nike in athletic shoes, and Jeff Bezos and Amazon in online marketplaces.

Apple is widely regarded as a company that relentlessly pushes the pace of innovation and as the most innovative company in the world. How many game-changing innovations has Apple come up with so far? Let's start counting: iPod, iTunes, iPhone, iMac, Apple Watch, and on we go.

The Innovator Mindset

The Innovator mindset is a great strategy for entrepreneurs who have a new idea that solves a problem or fulfills a need.

Today, technology is an industry where innovators abound. Many high-tech titans are serial innovators, such as Jack Dorsey, who pioneered Twitter, the short-text messaging platform, and Square, the portable payment system. Or Mark Zuckerberg, who created Facebook, the social network, and Meta, the metaverse company.

Charles Schwab identified the white space in the investing category, "discount trading." It was a first. A new concept in investing that attracted people who didn't want to pay high brokerage fees. Today, Charles Schwab is the largest discount brokerage firm.

The Eureka Moment

Most innovations occur not by happenstance or accident, but the Eureka moment comes from concentrated, active searching for a big idea.

The four Wharton students who launched Warby Parker, the online eyeglass company, were looking for a business idea for their computer lab class.[1] One of the team had just gotten new glasses and asked the group, "Why are prescription glasses so expensive?" and "Why couldn't they be made inexpensively and sold on the internet?

Most innovations don't happen spontaneously,
but through actively seeking a big idea

Their epiphany came when they discovered that there was a monopoly. One company controlled a 60–80 percent market share in eyeglasses. That's why eyeglasses were so expensive and ripe for disruption. The team named the company "Warby Parker" after two characters created by the author Jack Kerouac. A key ingredient of the company's success is its giveback program. For each pair of glasses sold, a pair is given to a person in need.

The Company Problem Solver

Every company has problems to be solved, and being the person who comes up with a creative solution can position you as a driver of your company's success.

Peter, a colleague who worked for a global financial services company, had extra time during the pandemic. So he conducted a remote listening tour, engaging with clients on how the bank could service them better. His engagement with clients led to a new type of research report that met clients' needs better than competitive reports.

While not a breakthrough invention, it was innovative all the same. It gave Peter a stronger relationship with his clients and brought recognition to him and to his company. Peter became the go-to person for solving problems in his company.

From Jet Lag to Energy Booster

A lot of times innovators tinker with something that already exists and reimagine something completely different, like Austrian consumer products salesperson Dietrich Mateschitz.[2]

On a business trip to Thailand, Mateschitz discovered a local Thai drink called Krating Daeng (literally Red Water Buffalo) that miraculously cured his jet lag. Mateschitz saw the potential for the drink in the West, with a few important modifications.

He named the drink Red Bull, a loose translation of the Thai name. He put the drink in a small thin can, not the standard beverage can, to convey the message that there's really strong stuff inside. He used the original Thai drink recipe, with one essential change for a Western audience—he added carbonation.

Positioning Is Everything

Mateschitz's real genius though was positioning Red Bull as a first, Strategy No. 1 Innovator.

He didn't position Red Bull as refreshing or energizing (Strategy No. 5 Attribute positioning). He didn't position it after the key users he was targeting, young men looking for an energy boost (Strategy No. 7 Target Market). He didn't position his new drink as a Thai beverage (Strategy No. 9 Heritage). Or employ Strategy No. 5 having a special formula and ingredients.

Mateschitz could have used any of these positioning strategies, but he had a better idea.

Creating a First

Mateschitz didn't want to simply introduce a new beverage brand. He set his sights higher and positioned himself as an innovator who invented a new category he called "energy drinks." He put "energy drink" prominently on the front of each can under the logo of the charging, red bulls.

If you can't be first in what exists,
create a new category you can be first in

Red Bull is still the market leader worldwide today in energy drinks. With as much caffeine as a cup of strong coffee, a can of Red Bull is all about energy and the performance edge it gives you. As the tagline says, "Red Bull Gives You Wings."

An Innovator Shaping Her Future

Sara Blakely is an important innovator, as many women will attest. She created the first wildly successful body-slimming shaper undergarments. Kim Kardashian later followed in her footsteps with a similar shaper line called SKIMS.

I love Sara Blakely's story. She was a 27-year-old, door-to-door fax machine salesperson in Atlanta, Georgia, but she was frustrated with her job. She wrote in her journal: "I want to invent a product I can sell to millions of people that will make them feel good." Like many innovators, she was actively looking to create something new.[3]

She found her big idea as only a woman could. Most women's slimming underwear at the time was uncomfortable and left lines and bulges that showed through your clothes.

Blakely had a new pair of figure-fitting, cream-colored pants that was languishing unworn in her closet because of that problem.

Then a lightbulb came on. Blakely got out a pair of control-top pantyhose, cut the feet out, and slipped the footless pantyhose on underneath her cream pants. She looked fabulous. No visible bulges.

The Innovator's Dilemma

Blakely decided to patent her shapewear idea and started doing research on hosiery mills. She discovered that most were located in North Carolina, and she started calling them.

Everyone hung up the phone when they heard her idea. Blakely didn't give up. She was an innovator, after all. So she drove to North Carolina to pitch hosiery mills in person.

People asked her, "What company are you with?" And she said, "Sara Blakely."

Then they asked, "Well, who do you have financial backing with?" And she said "Sara Blakely."

All the hosiery mills turned her down. They thought her shaper concept was a stupid idea. Then she got a call from the head of one mill, who told her, "I'll make your crazy idea."

She asked him, "Why did you change your mind?"

He said, "I have two daughters who think it's a good idea."

The rest is history. Sara Blakely named her shapewear Spanx and became the world's youngest self-made, female billionaire. Spanx, her innovative idea for women's shapewear, is now a publicly traded company.

5 Superpowers of Innovators

1. **Forward Thinking, Visionary with Clear Objectives:** Innovative leaders generate creative ideas but are also critical thinkers. They see opportunities that others miss. On top of trends and the latest research, they are constantly looking to enhance and improve what they're working on.

2. **Brilliant at Creative Problem Solving:** Innovators are full of ideas and in pursuit of solutions. They find challenging projects hard to resist and don't like to quit until they have achieved their goal. The rumor is that, on his death bed, Albert Einstein was trying to solve a problem.

3. **Bold Risk Takers:** Easily the most creative of the 10 Positioning Strategies, innovators are risk takers who avoid routine assignments. They like to imagine the possibilities, take a chance, and turn their imaginings into reality. They view failure as a learning opportunity, and that kind of positive thinking drives them forward.

4. **Fresh Thinking:** Everyone talks about thinking outside the box, but innovators really do. Innovators often diverge from the norm in their thinking and lifestyle. The important thing is, they're not hampered by what other people think. Innovators can be impulsive and change their minds a lot, which only serves to heighten their creativity.

5. **First to Invent Something:** Many Innovators are the first to invent something and some are even serial entrepreneurs, always keen to embark on new ventures.

Best Careers for Innovators

Innovators abound in technology and entrepreneurial ventures, especially in tech startups, where creating new products and services that fill a need in the marketplace are critical. Innovators are excellent problem solvers and creative thinkers. They are important contributors in companies in all industries and of all sizes, particularly in R&D and product development.

Exercise: Innovator Personal Brand Statement

Competitive Analysis

- **Identify and analyze two or three innovators** in your industry, company, or selected arena.
- **What sets you apart as an innovator?** Write down your thoughts.

Target Audience

- **Identify who you want to reach:** Be specific, such as your boss, colleagues, customers, job search contacts, industry leaders, the media, etc.
- **What problem can your creativity solve?** Write down your ideas.

Sample Positioning Statement

An innovative professional in an industry beset by mergers and dynamic change positioned herself in the following way.

Draft Sentence: For <u>senior managers, boss, clients, industry</u> who need <u>new products and services</u> I stand for <u>innovative problem solver in industries undergoing massive change.</u>

Final Sample Positioning Statement:

An innovator specializing in the converging worlds of technology, media, and communication.

Your Innovator Positioning Statement

Use the format below to explore Innovator positioning for Brand You by putting together a draft statement.

Draft Statement: For (<u>target audience</u>) who needs (<u>problem you solve</u>) I stand for (<u>value proposition</u>)

Final Innovator Positioning Statement

- **Identify three reasons to believe:** List innovative projects and accomplishments, books, articles, papers, awards, and experiences that support positioning yourself as an innovator.
- **List three keywords:** Select three adjectives or short keyword phrases that define you as an innovative problem solver.

The Innovator Brand in a Nutshell

Innovator Brand Idea: Innovative problem solver

Brand personality: Creative, risk taker

Values: Future oriented, creating new and better products and services

Motivation: Making a difference, improving way things are done

Ideal customers: People who value new products and services

Battle cry: Onward and upward!

Chapter 5

Positioning Strategy No. 2 Leader

L eadership is the winningest strategy for brands.

The leader—the brand with the highest market share in a category—has on average two times the market share as the number-two brand. So it's an envious positioning to claim. Once established, leaders are hard to knock from their perch because of the link people make between the market leader being the "best" brand in its category.

Leadership is a winning positioning for people, too. Being the leader of your team, department, company, or group means that you are recognized for your accomplishments and your role in leading people and keeping them focused until they cross the finish line.

The best leaders have a clear mission that unites their team around a common goal. They are quick to adapt to a crisis with honest, realistic information, empathy, and a game plan.

People will see you differently when you are a leader. You must be better than someone in a subordinate role because you were chosen to lead the charge, is how the thinking goes. People want to hear from you. They want to know your point of view, your priorities, your strategy.

In a world clouded by conflict and change, leaders are more important than ever. Whether it's in business, government, or organizations, we admire leaders not just for their accomplishments and title, but for their ability to inspire us to tackle big challenges and achieve great things. Leaders always have a plan.

Are You a Leader?

Is your strength your ability to motivate and lead people?

Are you energized working with people to achieve important goals?

Can you tie specific accomplishments to your leadership?

Do people seek your direction and guidance to overcome challenges?

If there's a crisis, do you step in and fill the void?

If you answered yes to two or more of these questions, then you should consider brand Strategy No. 2 Leader. The world needs more people just like you.

> **Leader Positioning: I am a leader of _____**
> **and my goal as a leader is _____**

The Leader Personality

You stand out because you are confident and competent and you motivate others in good times and, especially, in challenging times.

You believe in yourself and know what you want to achieve. You are goal-oriented and believe in your ability to perform well and exceed expectations. You inspire others and believe that you have what it takes to motivate and lead others to achieve, even exceed, goals.

You have high self-esteem that is closely connected to your accomplishments and success. You are assertive. You project strength and tend to ignore or downplay feelings of weakness and vulnerability. You realize that you lose credibility if you equivocate.

You're most fulfilled when leading a team to achieve important goals. You seek action and stimulation, and you're an excellent planner in overseeing complex projects. You can feel constant pressure to take on more responsibility, and you genuinely want to take it all on. It's okay, because you're driven and thrive on the visibility and attention being a leader gives you.

As a leader, you feel comfortable speaking with authority, and your followers respond to your call to action. In fact, competitors often study your actions and words. But you're not perfect. You can be aggressive and impulsive.

Most of the time you:	*But sometimes you:*
■ Are energetic and competitive	■ Make others feel pressured
■ Are a strong team motivator	■ Can be aggressive
■ Attract attention as a leader for your accomplishments	■ Don't seem to care about others
Generally people see you as:	*But you can:*
■ Successful and confident	■ Be too demanding
■ A planner, on top of everything	■ Criticize others
■ A big picture thinker	■ Avoid change and new ideas

If this sounds like you, all the more reason to explore Positioning Strategy No. 2 Leader.

Follow The Leader

Many people believe that the number-one brand must be "better" (better quality, better performance, better tasting, better looking, etc., depending on the category) because more people buy it.

That's why when a brand has a leadership claim, marketers brag about it and promote it heavily as "the leading brand chosen by more people." It's a persuasive message, so even more people buy it.

Marketers can charge a higher price for the market leader too. And customers are willing to pay it because of the trust they have in the leading brand.

Make Your Mark

You'll benefit from being a leader, too. People will make positive assumptions about you and your abilities. You're likely to be paid more. You will be harder to dislodge from your leadership role, too.

Leadership has a halo effect
People assume you're "better" than people in a non-leadership role

---

Of course, you can't build your leadership claim with smoke and mirrors. You must have specific accomplishments you can tie to your leadership of your team. You have to be able to answer the questions "What's my goal for the organization?" and "What makes my leadership different?"

Culture and Action

You create a strong bond with your people just like leading brands have with their loyal customers. Your goal is to create a special culture of people who are inspired by your leadership to accomplish remarkable goals.

You're good at supervising big projects and getting the right people in place to implement long-term strategies not just short-term goals.

That's why successful leaders are likely to be powerful communicators and listeners who can inspire others with the right message.

Public Opinion Baths

Strong leaders understand the emotional needs of their followers. President Abraham Lincoln would set aside several hours in the morning to hear the needs of regular people who stood outside his office.

Many were seeking favors. Others wanted to influence him on an issue, and some just merely wanted to greet him.

Lincoln's staff wanted him to stop his morning sessions, telling him it was a waste of his time. Yet Lincoln wanted to know how ordinary people felt about him and his policies.

His encounters with real people gave him a way to gauge public opinion, way before instant political polling came about. Lincoln called his daily meetings with regular folks his "public opinion baths."[1] His encounters helped him craft his messages during the Civil War.

First in the Hearts

In the early days of setting up the republic, there was a lot of disagreement about what the new government of the United States should look like. But there was no disagreement among the founders about the person to lead the new republic.

George Washington was the unanimous choice.

As a Revolutionary War hero, Washington was known not just as a brilliant war strategist and planner, but as a leader who inspired his soldiers with his courage in battle, his integrity, and the trust he engendered. He often spoke to his troops about their sacrifice.

In his first two years as president, he hit the road on a listening tour visiting every state in the fledgling country to learn firsthand the concerns of his countrymen. That's why today, when you travel around the Northeast of the United States, you see a lot of signs that say, "George Washington Slept Here." It's probably true.

He was, as American patriot Henry Lee wrote, "First in war, first in peace, and first in the hearts of his countrymen."

But you'd be wrong if you think that the first president wasn't adept at personal branding. Biographers point out that Washington had fierce military and political ambitions and cared deeply about his reputation and succeeding at every stage of his career.

Look the Part

Washington's physical presence was extraordinary, according to many contemporaneous reports.[2] Part of it was his height. He was tall, at six feet, two inches. John Adams was five feet, seven inches. James Madison was only five feet, four inches. Only Thomas Jefferson was as tall as Washington.

Washington had charisma and executive presence. Contemporaries describe him as "muscular," "strong," "well-proportioned," and "manly and bold." They also said he "inspires confidence" and had a "graceful gait and gestures" and the "smile of benevolence."

Such was Washington's impact that crowded rooms went silent and people stopped talking when he entered the room, according to written records.

Abigail Adams, wife of his vice president, John Adams, praised him as "polite with dignity, affable without familiarity, distant without Haughtyness, Grave without Austerity, Modest, Wise, & Good."

Washington understood the branding power of clothes and appearance and cared about how he looked, down to every detail. One biographer cites a memo to his tailor specifying "the number of buttonholes in his coat, its length and the width of the lapels." Whether rallying the troops in the battlefield or in comporting himself in the halls of the Capitol, Washington was on brand.

Leader vs. Number Two

New leaders often discover that leadership means leaving your comfort zone and taking charge. On her first large leadership role, my colleague Daren sent her new boss a detailed memo on how she planned to revamp the department in the aftermath of the pandemic. She wanted to get his okay before announcing it to her new staff.

Her boss called her up and said, "I don't buy a dog and bark for it too." What he meant was, *I hired you to run the business. You're in charge. You make your own decisions. Don't expect me to do your job.*

Daren quickly realized that she wasn't a number two anymore. As they say, "It's better to ask for forgiveness than ask for permission." She was running the show now.

Best Leadership Claim

In the branding world, every category has a leader board, and being the number one in sales is what counts.

But there are a lot of different ways of defining sales leadership. You just have to find a niche where you can be number one.

Look at the car category. A car brand can be the overall leader as the best-selling car in America (Toyota). Or you can be the leader of part of the car market, say the top-selling luxury car (BMW) or the leader in SUVs (Toyota RAV4), and on and on. All of these car makers can make a leadership claim on a segment of the market. It's valuable because prospective buyers often follow leadership rankings in making purchase decisions.

Slice and dice until you
find a niche where you can be the leader

Likewise, there are lots of ways to segment your arena to make a leadership claim. Let's say you're in sales. You might be the leader in sales overall at your company or the leader in sales in a segment of the market or with a particular type of client.

Or you could be the leader in a geographic area or in a specific product line. Or as one sales leader told me, "I am the sales leader with the fewest but the most profitable accounts."

You could be an emerging leader by volunteering to lead an ad hoc project or heading up an employee resource group at your company.

The Leadership Hierarchy

There is a connection between power and rank. If you lead a team of fifty, people will assume you are better than someone supervising a mere five people. So there's constant pressure on the leader to advance up the food chain.

If you're the CEO of one of the Fortune 100 companies, like Tim Cook at Apple, aren't you better than someone heading up a company at the other end of the Fortune 500 list? Likewise, the higher you rank in the hierarchy of your organization, the greater the power you are perceived to have.

The more people you lead,
the greater your perceived power

As a leader, you're at the forefront of the new developments in your industry. You have money for big projects. The media wants to hear your point of view.

You'll be under more scrutiny, too. As much as the media can help a leader build a brand and speed up your career trajectory, it can also destroy your brand image, practically overnight. But there's always the opportunity for a redemption story.

Great Expectations for Leaders

A sea change seems to be taking place in the expectations people have for business leaders.

Today it isn't just about increasing shareholder value. More people are looking to businesses to step in and help solve many of today's challenges, such as racism, climate change, digital privacy, voting rights, and information reliability, according to the Edelman Trust Barometer study in 2021.[3] The study shows that business is not only the most trusted institution among the four studied, but it is also the only institution seen as both ethical and competent.

It's called *stakeholder capitalism*, the idea that companies should not just be run to enrich shareholders. We're increasingly seeing business leaders involved in a broader range of interests—local communities, the environment, employees—and their non-business activities are changing how they are perceived as leaders.

The expectation is that business leaders can solve important social issues by applying the same results orientation that they bring to leading a business.

The Empathetic Leader

Mary Barra is a first—the first female CEO of a major automaker and the first female leader of the prestigious Business Roundtable. As is the case with many firsts, Mary Barra is fascinating.

She's a female leader of General Motors, a Fortune 50 company, in a real guy-oriented business—cars. A company lifer, she's moving the lumbering, gigantic GM into electric cars, creating the first truly mass-market, all-electric car. She has vowed that GM will be all electric by 2035.[4]

Empathy and collaboration are typically
associated with the female style of leadership

Barra's style of leadership is one of empathy, collaboration, and eagerness to give credit to her team.

She constantly asks for feedback from her staff. It's a more collaborative and democratic leadership style, in contrast to the more top-down hierarchical style of leadership more associated with men.

Empathy is important in a crisis, and Barra was recognized for her active communication with employees during the Covid-19 pandemic. She retooled a production line to build ventilators when they were in short supply for Covid patients. During the crisis she also cut the cost structure and the time it takes to get things done inside General Motors.

Crisis Defines a Leader

A number of analysts have cited women heads of state as outperforming male leaders during the Covid-19 pandemic, such as the former German Chancellor Angela Merkel and New Zealand Prime Minister Jacinda Ardern.

Ardern's first crisis was in the mass shooting at two mosques in Christchurch, New Zealand, in 2019.[5] She immediately shared heartfelt compassion for the victims, condemned the hate talk of the shooter, and affirmed the country's values.

Later she took action by changing the country's gun laws.

During the pandemic, Ardern was also praised for her leadership. In March of 2020, she addressed her citizens from the prime minister's office, last used for a major announcement almost 40 years earlier. So the locale signaled the unusual importance and urgency of her message.

She spoke of the pandemic with empathy and specifics, outlining her preemptive strategy to "fight by going hard and going early." Ardern won reelection as prime minister in a record-breaking landslide in October 2020.

The World's Last Global Monarch

Queen Elizabeth II is the oldest and longest reigning English monarch.

At a time when hereditary monarchies are not popular, the popularity of Elizabeth II is amazing. And she's amazing to behold in her brightly colored coats and matching hats as she speaks of duty and courage in the face of difficulty in her public addresses.

Elizabeth II is the epitome of royalty. She's polite, reserved, and obedient to the constitutional mandate of her reign. She has all the trappings of royalty—the regalia, palaces, jewels, and ceremonial pageantry.

Yet she seems down-to-earth and interacts well with ordinary people. I watched her getting a case of the giggles speaking via Zoom to the Jamaican bobsled team who were training in the UK before they set off to compete in the 2022 Olympics in Beijing.

There is also the feeling that she is not just a steady hand at the wheel, but a savvy leader. She insisted on personally driving Crown Prince Abdullah, of Saudi Arabia, the leader of a country that didn't allow women to drive at the time, when he visited her at Balmoral, Scotland.

The Voice of Authority

Many studies suggest that low, "masculine" voices are an asset to leaders. Most male CEOs measure at the average male range of 125.5 Hz. Male voices at the deeper range tend to earn more and lead bigger companies.[6]

In one study of men and women, people with a low pitch were perceived as having a higher social rank and viewed as more dominant.[7]

The power of a low-pitched voice was not lost on former UK prime minister Margaret Thatcher. When she underwent vocal coaching to sound more authoritative, she reportedly lowered her voice's pitch an amazing 60 Hz.[8]

Who can forget Gillian Anderson's portrayal of the Iron Lady in *The Crown*? It was the voice—the low pitch, the slow cadence, the theatrical way she spoke—more than the immovable helmet hair style or the power suits that projected the leadership power of Margaret Thatcher.

5 Super Powers of Leaders

1. **Sets a Vision That Shapes an Organization:** Leaders set a purpose, a vision, and a common goal for their team. Leaders are clear about why the organization exists and how it contributes to society.
2. **Motivational Speaker Who Inspires Employees:** Leaders are professional inspirers who motivate teams to reach their potential, making sure to acknowledge and appreciate team and individual accomplishments.
3. **Adapt Quickly in a World of Rapid Change:** Leaders have an exceptional ability to adapt to change in a world of rapid innovation. While leaders take a long-term view, they are able to pivot when unexpected change occurs.
4. **Track Record of Accomplishments:** Leaders are goal oriented and they set high standards for themselves and assemble a tapestry of experiences and accomplishments to hone their leadership skills.
5. **Exceptional Planning:** Solving problems and overseeing complex plans are in a leader's DNA. Leaders realize the importance of setting goals and supervising detailed action plans to achieve them.

Exercise: Leader Personal Brand Statement

Competitive Analysis

- **Identify key leaders:** In your industry, company, or selected arena
- **What sets you apart as a leader?** Write down your thoughts.

Target Audience

- **Identify whom you want to reach:** Be specific, such as your boss, colleagues, customers, job search contacts, industry leaders, the media, etc.
- **What problem do you solve as a leader?** Write down your ideas.

Sample Positioning Statement

Example: A leader felt his differentiator was his team-building and sales skills during the pandemic.

Draft Sentence: For <u>senior managers, team members</u> who need <u>to get teams to be productive,</u> I stand for <u>being a strong leader in achieving next-level sales success during time of change.</u>

Final Sample Positioning Statement:

Motivating next-level sales success is my DNA.

Your Leader Positioning Statement: Use the format below to explore Innovator positioning for Brand You, by putting together a draft statement:

Draft Statement: For (<u>target audience</u>) who needs (<u>problem you solve</u>) I stand for (<u>value proposition</u>)

Final Leader Positioning Statement _____

- **Identify three reasons to believe:** List leadership projects and accomplishments, books, articles, papers, awards, and experiences that support positioning yourself as a leader.
- **List three keywords:** Select three adjectives or short keyword phrases that define you as a leader.

Leader Brand in a Nutshell

Leader Brand Idea: Strong inspirational leader of people

Keyword: Leadership

Values: Accomplishing goals, building a strong team, leaving a legacy

Motivation: Strong desire to make your mark in the world

Brand voice: Authoritative, confident

Ideal customers: People who admire a strong leader who inspires teams

Battle cry: We will meet any challenge.

Chapter 6

Positioning Strategy No. 3 Maverick

As much as business titans, political leaders, and celebrities are part of the mythology of most cultures, so are underdogs. (Think Tom Cruise as Pete "Maverick" Mitchell in *Top Gun: Maverick*.)

We have a soft spot for the rebel—the lone defiers of convention, the irreverent ones who don't follow the rules but accomplish remarkable things, the outliers who cut their own path and succeed. We admire the mavericks.

Maverick positioning is also called *Opposite-, Versus-,* or *Reverse Positioning*. Executing this positioning is simplicity itself: Everything the traditional leader stands for in your industry, you are the opposite (within reason).

As a maverick, you are hardwired for challenge, the more ambitious the better. It's easy to follow what everyone else is doing. You don't believe that success comes from doing the expected. In fact, you inspire others with your freewheeling style.

You make bureaucrats nervous because of your philosophy "If it ain't broken . . . break it." You are known for having contrary points of view and being a free thinker. But you are not out there without supporters. There's always a market for an opposite point of view.

Are You a Maverick?

Are you the opposite of the traditional person in your career role?

Do you have an unconventional approach or point of view?

Are you willing to take risks to achieve your goals?

Do you stand out from others?

Are you highly creative with lots of ideas and goals?

If you answered yes to two or more of these questions, then you may want to position yourself using Strategy No. 3, the Maverick.

Maverick Positioning: I am the opposite of the traditional person in my role because _____

The Maverick Personality

As a maverick, you have a contrary mindset, an unconventional way of thinking that's not fond of the status quo. You're a challenger to the old guard. It takes guts to go against the grain, and you have guts in spades.

You tend to feel separate from others, and your outsider perspective and self-sufficiency leads to independent thinking. Many mavericks weren't great students, or only did well in courses they were interested in.

You attract other people who admire your unique, even quirky, personality, and you are fascinated by offbeat people as well. You are confident enough to avoid following the established path. Rather, you seek out the road less traveled as your path to success.

You have lots of ideas and big goals. You tend to be a goal-oriented risk taker with a strong desire to succeed. You are likely to be an engaging storyteller who uses story to sell your ideas, point of view, and benefits.

You're a disrupter who feels comfortable turning things upside down and inside out. People see you as a master of cunning. You know how to energize your message with bold gestures and unusual stories to captivate your audience.

You can be aggressive, egocentric, and disagreeable, but you are also extroverted, lively, and spontaneous. And, at times, a tad eccentric. You don't mind looking and thinking differently from the norm and are attracted to contrarian thinkers like you.

Most of the time you:	*But sometimes you:*
■ Are spontaneous and lively	■ Are overly aggressive
■ Take risks to achieve goals	■ Dislike conformists
■ Challenge the status quo	■ Can be egocentric

Generally people see you as:	*But you can:*
■ Unconventional	■ Be too wild
■ A calculated risk taker	■ Go too far
■ Unique	■ Be too self-centered

If this sounds like you, all the more reason to explore Positioning Strategy No. 3 Maverick.

Be the Opposite

For every Microsoft, there's an Apple. For every Bill Gates, there's a Steve Jobs. For every Mary Barra, there's an Elon Musk.

If established leaders think X, you think Y. If they wear a business suit, you wear jeans and a T-shirt (think Mark Zuckerberg and Jack Dorsey). If your competitors are big and corporate, you're nimble and entrepreneurial.

The Power of Contrast

People and things stand out when they are the opposite of what's traditional or expected. That's the power of the maverick. You're a challenger brand. A famous example of this strategy is the Avis rent-a-car campaign from the early 1960s. Avis was having trouble competing in a world dominated by Hertz.

Hertz was by far the leader in car rental at the time, until Avis came up with the legendary opposite positioning line, "When you're only No. 2, you try harder." Avis car rentals went through the roof.

Another classic maverick positioning campaign is the one Apple launched in 2006 featuring the cool Mac hipster ("I'm a Mac") and the PC guy wearing baggy khakis ("I'm a PC"). Who did you identify with?

Breath of Fresh Air

If traditional leaders talk in scripted, carefully measured words at press conferences, you are more likely to get into dustups on Twitter with your tell-it-like-it-is point of view.

If the establishment leader is a bit dull and circumspect, you're interesting and bold. Look at Jack Dorsey, head of financial services company Block (formerly Square). He changed his title from CEO to Block head in 2022.

Mavericks are rule breakers. You don't necessarily see winning as a civilized affair won by following the rules. Au contraire.

Got it? We can go on and on. In almost every way you, the maverick, are the antidote to the traditional person in your line of work.

David Against Goliath

You're a challenger brand, and coming from behind makes your victory all the more precious. The odds may be against you, but you have fans who are rooting for you, the maverick underdog, just the same.

You are different. You have courage to set yourself apart from the tried-and-true routine. You are your own person.

People are attracted to you due to your outlier status. After all, mavericks are living the life most of us don't dare emulate.

Passionate Idea Generator

You excite others with your creativity and enthusiasm. You don't like slipping into routine or following familiar strategies or procedures.

You can make bureaucrats and traditionalists nervous. In fact, you can be counted on to challenge the traditional way of doing things. You know you can come up with something better than the status quo.

As an underdog, you are often not at the top of the food chain, but your lower rank doesn't hamper your success. It enhances it.

Intense Work Ethic

You are goal oriented and get results. Sometimes you can be too risky or go too far and have to be reined in, especially if you work at a conservative company.

That's why maverick leaders thrive in an entrepreneurial environment. Competitive by nature, you like to reposition competitors by turning their strengths into weaknesses.

Your pitch may go something like this: "Who would you rather go with, the bigger, more experienced-but-living-in-the-past choice, or a smaller, nimble, and cutting-edge company who will take you into the future?"

Not Afraid of Controversy

A defining characteristic of mavericks is having contrary views or at least a different point of view than most people have in your industry. Your ability to create "news" or controversy has make you a darling of the media.

Reporters know that you're unlikely to say, "No comment." They can count on you for a quotable quip or at least a fresh spin on issues affecting your industry or even the broader world. At meetings you are not afraid to suggest an alternative way of doing something. You think questioning the status quo is necessary.

Clothes That Talk

Alexandria Ocasio-Cortez, known in branding shorthand as AOC, is a maverick politician known not just for her progressive politics but for her bold, message-rich personal style.

A former bartender, AOC made history in 2018 as the youngest woman to be elected to the US Congress, at age 29. In a matter of months, she became the most well-known member of Congress and one of the most talked-about people in politics, with an immense following on social media.

She's changing the dress code of politics. Her signature style includes bright red lipstick (Stilo Beso), hoop earrings, and fashionable clothes.

Sometimes her clothes are on message, like when she wears white in honor of the suffragists.

Sometimes subtlety flies out the window, and her clothes have the message written right on them. At the Met Museum Gala in 2021, AOC raised eyebrows when she wore a white gown with "Tax the rich" in bold red letters on the back. "The medium is the message," she posted on Instagram in response to criticism.

If you think and live outside the box, maverick positioning might be for you.

Maverick Prototype

Steve Jobs is the prototype of the maverick leader. Known for his trademark black, mock turtleneck shirts and blue jeans, Jobs didn't dress or lead like your typical CEO. He popularized dressing down for big events among tech leaders.

Mavericks like Jobs honestly believe that traditional leaders are misguided. He saw himself as the anti-leader, saying, "I never wanted to be a businessman, because all the businessmen I knew I didn't want to be like."[1]

Jobs cast Apple as an underdog in the early days. He described the competition with IBM as a struggle with the "evil empire" for "freedom" and against "mind control."

He rejected bland and geeky tech design as ugly, and transformed the tech industry. He meticulously focused on a minimalistic aesthetic on a long series of history-altering products like the MacBook, iPhone, and iPod.

Practice Practice Practice

All the focus at Apple was on Jobs, and he delivered. Jobs was a spellbinding showman and master of the keynote address. Every product launch was brilliantly choreographed. Every move, every slide, every image carefully planned.

Jobs left nothing to chance, even the parts he wanted to appear unscripted. At the end of a presentation, just when you think it was all over, Jobs casually says, like an afterthought, "One more thing," and pulls another rabbit out of the hat. And that ending gambit became part of his trademark presentation format.

Jobs rehearsed over and over again. That's why he was so good.

The Ego of the Maverick

Jobs saw himself as a genius apart from 99.9% of the world. He was a demanding leader who probably broke most of the rules taught in business school. You had to prove yourself every day, or you were out. Yet Jobs attracted a loyal following of people who were almost like members of cult, with Jobs as guru and employees and customers entranced by his vision of how he would change the world.

As others have noticed, Apple's famous "The Crazy Ones" commercial could be describing Jobs himself: "To the crazy ones. Here's to the misfits. The rebels. The troublemakers. The people who see the world differently. The people who are crazy enough to believe they can change the world are the ones who actually do." Apple's battle cry says it all: "Think Different."

The Virgin Attitude

Richard Branson is known for his rule-breaking approach to leadership, saying that he never learned any rules so he can be called a rule breaker.

His maverick bona fides start with the saucy name he gave to his company. Branson chose the name, Virgin, for his first mail-order record company, because he and his partners were "virgins in business."

No doubt Branson had an ulterior motive. The name gave him a PR platform from the early days. Even decades later, the media still likes to ask him, "How did you come up with the Virgin name?"

Not a Fan of Suits

Branson doesn't look like your typical multi-national corporate leader, with his longish hair, trendy clothes, and deep tan.

He looks like he just stepped off his yacht, not just spent the day running a global conglomerate.

In fact, these days Branson might have just gotten off his yacht, since he's not the CEO of any of his companies anymore, a surprising fact. Branson delegates the boring day-to-day stuff to very capable people so he can focus on the fun stuff like PR.

Class Clown PR Strategy

Branson is the face of the company and known for his *anything goes* PR strategy.[2] There's no limit to the stunts he'll do and how far he'll go to promote Virgin's companies. He's put on lipstick and a wedding gown to publicize his retail store, Virgin Brides. He's gone up-up-and-away in a hot-air balloon as an attention-getting publicity stunt to circumnavigate the world.

Branson's battle cry: "Break the rules with a Virgin attitude" is a classic maverick point of view.

The Wow Appeal of the Maverick

Like many mavericks, much of the fascination we have with Tesla and SpaceX is Musk himself. He's interesting. He's a showman. He's contrary. He's a genius. He's the richest man in the world. What's next?

Musk's brilliance and image as a controversy-courting tech renegade have made him a media star. He is only the second billionaire to host *Saturday Night Live* (after Donald Trump), and *SNL* has been around for over 45 years.

Musk has over 80 million devoted fans on Twitter, making him Twitter's most followed tech entrepreneur. In 2022, he made a bid to buy Twitter. He can seem to delight or dismay depending on his mood. It's easy to wonder, What's he going to do next?"[3]

A Buzz Machine

Musk changed his title from CEO to "Technoking of Tesla." He always seems to turn up in the news cycle. There's always buzz going on about him, with his audacious goals like establishing a colony on Mars. He's encouraging people to have more children and doing his bit. He named his seventh child (a boy) XAE A-Xii, and his eighth child (a girl) Exa Dark Siderael.

He's often in fights with the establishment and seems to see the world as David (or rather Elon) versus Goliath.

Innovator or Maverick?

Musk is so talented as an innovator that we could easily put him in the Positioning Strategy No. 1 Innovator.

His electric car company, Tesla, transformed the electric car industry. His company SpaceX is the first private company to launch a man into space, and the first to send ordinary people into orbit. He created the first reusable booster rocket.

But Musk's unconventional point of view and outsized personality puts him squarely in the Maverick positioning camp. Musk is a can-do leader. His battle cry: "If no one else does it, I will."

5 Superpowers of Mavericks

1. **A Contrary or Fresh Perspective:** Mavericks are not afraid to have viewpoints that are different or even controversial. But you don't have to be a radical contrarian to be a maverick. You just need a fresh view point or one that has a different twist on conventional wisdom.

2. **Different Image and Leadership Style:** Mavericks are not old guard. They often are easy to spot, since their self-presentation often is dramatic and not like the executive presence of traditional leaders. (Think Richard Branson, Lady Gaga, and tussle-haired Boris Johnson.) Mavericks generally don't follow traditional leadership rules, but it doesn't matter. They tend to attract employees and followers who relish their out-of-the-ordinary point of view and renegade, even roguish, image.

3. **Entrepreneurial, Creative Mindset:** Mavericks are natural entrepreneurs, dynamic and gung-ho, full of ideas and ambition. They are highly creative and tend to set challenging goals. They have an intense work ethic and are relentless until they achieve results. Many mavericks are serial entrepreneurs, given their inclination to embark on new ventures.

4. **Highly Visible and Controversial:** Mavericks often take a keen interest in their personal brand and in marketing themselves. They are masters of cunning. Getting into and out of scrapes is one of their defining skills.

5. **Master of the Quotable Quip:** Mavericks tend to be darlings of the media since they provide a lot of interesting ink for journalists. They are often bold and dramatic speakers at meetings big or small. They can be sought-after speakers at industry conferences and panels because of their different take on what's happening in their industry.

Best Careers for Mavericks

Independent spirits abound in technology and entrepreneurial ventures, especially in tech startups where mavericks can feel under threat by the Big Tech monopoly and use a David versus Goliath PR strategy.

Writers, artists, performers, and creative people are often mavericks by choice and personality. Performers like Lady Gaga, Billie Eilish, and Bob Dylan understand the power of standing apart with a maverick brand. Many mavericks thrive as media pundits and consultants where being the antidote of the traditional view is valuable.

Mavericks are often seen as a welcome disrupter and game changer. People are attracted to their bold, unconventional, sometimes-irreverent wisdom. Think of the maverick chef, Anthony Bourdain, who was not just a guide to food but to the wider world. That' why we miss him so much.

The Maverick strategy can be risky, especially if you work in a large corporation, but many have mavericks in departments where creativity is critical, like marketing and product development. Though mavericks are not a good fit in conservative work environments, where they can be viewed as reckless and not appropriate.

Exercise: Maverick Personal Brand Statement

Competitive Analysis

- **Identify the leaders in your competitive set and what they stand for:** In your industry, company, or selected arena

- **Determine the opposite:** How can you establish a different point of view, image, and set of accomplishments for your maverick positioning?

Target Audience

- **Identify who you want to reach:** Be specific, such as your boss, colleagues, customers, etc. Visualize their identity, personality, values, and lifestyle.
- **What problem do you solve for them?** Write down your thoughts.

Sample Positioning Statement

Example: A corporate finance employee who wanted to move to a creative position in digital marketing wanted to rebrand himself as a maverick and who was both creative and analytical.

Initial sentence: For (senior managers at top digital companes) who needs (a creative problem solver) I stand for (a rare combination: strong business chops and creative ability)

Final sample positioning sentence:

Mind of a Businessman and Soul of a Creative

Your Maverick Positioning Statement: Use the format below to explore maverick positioning for Brand You by putting together a draft statement.

Draft Statement: For (target audience) who needs (problem you solve) I stand for (value proposition)

Final Maverick Positioning Statement _____

- **Identify three reasons to believe:** List unconventional projects and accomplishments, point of view, books, articles, papers, awards, and experiences that support positioning yourself as a maverick
- **List three keywords:** Select three adjectives or short keyword phrases that define you as a maverick

The Maverick Brand in a Nutshell

Maverick Brand Idea: Bold, unconventional leader who gets results

Keyword: Contrary

Values: Achievement, risk-taking, independence

Motivation: Strong desire for change and challenging status quo

Brand voice: Tell it like it is, passionate

Ideas customers: People who like the thrill of an unconventional perspective

Battle cry: Defy the ordinary.

Chapter 7

Positioning Strategy No. 4 Attribute

The most common positioning strategy is to build a brand's identity around an attribute—a strength, characteristic, or quirk that sets your brand apart from competitors.

Every industry, every product area, every job is associated with attributes that are important. The attribute strategy is particularly popular in brand categories like cars where there are a lot of attributes that customers seek out.

Mercedes-Benz's brand is built around "prestige." BMW stands for "driving performance." Volvo's word is "safety," and on and on. That's why marketers talk in terms of "owning a word."

It's the same with people. You want to be associated with an attribute, a defining word that conveys your value added. It's your keyword. It's your superpower. You need an attribute that is important in your line of work, that is not associated with others and that is credible for you to own.

When you find that attribute, you make it the focus of your marketing and personal brand profile. It's what makes your brand most appealing. What you want is a strong tie between you and the word. So when people think of your attribute they think of you, and when they think of you, they think of the attribute.

Your job is to stake your claim on the *one attribute* that will appeal to your target audience and give you the best marketing leverage against competitors.

Forget about all the wonderful attributes people admire you for. You need to select one strength to hang your hat on and then build your brand around it. That way, people are more likely to pay attention to you and what you say.

Do You Identify with an Important Attribute?

What particular attributes, strengths, and characteristics do you have that set you apart from others?

What strengths and abilities do people compliment you on at work?

What successful initiatives or accomplishments were a result of a specific attribute?

What one attribute will give you maximum advantage with your target audience?

Is there anything peculiar about you that can be your attribute?

If you've got standout strength in one attribute that's important in what you do, then Strategy No. 4 Attribute positioning might be right for you.

> **Attribute Positioning: My attribute is** _____
> **and it's important because** _____

The Attribute Personality

The key ingredient of people who identify with a specific attribute is focus. You have a high degree of self-control and the ability to concentrate on your key strength without getting sidetracked. You build your narrative around your value proposition professionally. Your attribute is your superpower that sets you apart from others and is behind your success in the world. Your attribute is the nucleus of how you promote yourself with colleagues and customers.

You don't just select an attribute because it appeals to you. You are very intuitive and are able to identify the best attribute that "clicks" with the needs of your target audience and is authentic for you. Because you score high in empathy and intuition, you have the ability to read social cues, even subtle ones. You often go with your gut, and it is generally accurate.

You can easily alter your behavior and pitch in order to "fit in" to a specific social or professional situation. You are able to present yourself in socially and professionally desirable ways and adapt to new situations more effectively than others.

Most of the time you:	*But sometimes you:*
■ Maximize innate strengths ■ Stand for something that is important in your field ■ Build your value add around your differentiator	■ Can be too immersed in tasks ■ Argue for ideas you don't believe ■ Change your position to please people

Generally people see you as:	*But you can:*
■ Knowing your strengths ■ Able to "click" with others ■ Focused on what you're good at	■ Be fake or inauthentic ■ Mimic others so they like you ■ Be lacking in emotion

If this sounds like you, all the more reason to explore Positioning Strategy No. 4 and build your positioning around a key attribute.

What's Your Superpower?

Most people want to pile on lots of attributes. They want to be all things to all people so they have the best chance of success.

It's a mistake.

You'll confuse rather than attract interest in you and your abilities. It is difficult enough to link one attribute to a product or person. It's close to impossible to connect two or more. Besides, if you establish a breakout attribute, people won't think you're only good at one thing anyway.

Finding Your Attribute

Use attribute positioning to "identify" the best attribute that "clicks" with the needs of others and is a strength of yours. In short, your attribute is your value proposition.

Your attribute could be strategy, invention, know-how, motivator, connector, even personality traits like charisma and likability.

It's always smart to build off of what you already own in the minds of your target audience. Start with other people first. How do others see you? Do you know? If not, ask them.

You have the opportunity to pick up clues every day. What do people compliment you on at work? What do they criticize you for?

Then look inward. Put a blank piece of paper in front of you. What adjectives come to mind? What do you admire about yourself? How do you want others to see you?

Lock In Your Keyword (or Phrase)

What defining characteristic do you want others to link with you? Is there a way to build a connection with what's already in the minds of others to what you want to stand for?

Finally, think outward. What are the hot buttons in your industry or line of work? What strength is lacking at your company? How can you fill the gap?

When you find your word, you want to lock it in. Don't underestimate the power of repetition. The more you repeat an attribute or a message, the more likely others will associate you with it, like Dan did with his attribute.

An Attribute in Demand

An engineer by background, Dan was put in charge of a major department during the Covid-19 pandemic. Sales revenues were down. The industry and its customers were in a severe slump. Supply chain problems were holding up production.

It's often challenging times that provide an impetus to solve problems that have long been festering in a company. Dan's company didn't have good systems in place to manage its production schedule. So the supply chain problems were magnified and got out of control during the crisis. Problems were piling up. Not much was getting done.

No one was taking responsibility for the problems or finding solutions.

Dan decided to position himself around the attribute "accountability." It was an important attribute that colleagues and customers associated with him, with his strengths in planning, project management, problem solving, and taking ownership of his areas of responsibility.

Attribute as Battle Cry

The word "accountability" indicated that Dan wasn't just talking about systems and technology improvements. It demonstrated that there would be consequences if his team didn't start to take ownership of their areas.

He tied his word to his initiatives and in his battle cries to his team, such as "Accountability means solutions, not just problems" and "Everyone's accountable, everywhere all the time."

Other colleagues may be better than Dan in creativity, financial analysis, or marketing, but no one could match his ability to develop processes, technology, and metrics to track performance and accountability.

Tweaking Your Attribute

You may not get your attribute right at first. Happens to everyone, even to marketing powerhouses like Procter & Gamble.

When Pampers, the first disposable diaper, was launched in the 1960s, the Pampers marketing team focused on the attribute "convenience."

Convenience seemed perfect. With a paper disposable diaper, moms didn't have to clean and disinfect used cloth diapers or hire an expensive diaper service. They didn't have to carry stinky cloth diapers around if they had to use one on an outing.

Target Audience Knows Best

But the convenience attribute positioning didn't sit well with moms.

Moms felt guilty. They saw the choice in simple, black-and-white terms. Cloth diapers were best for babies. Disposable diapers were best for moms. Plus, Pampers were pricey. So moms voted with their hearts and pocketbooks. Sales were poor in the early days.

Then Pampers selected a different attribute. "Better absorbency." And P&G developed a cheaper manufacturing process and were able to lower the price.[1]

Now moms didn't have to feel bad about choosing Pampers. Absorbency was better for babies. Sales went sky high.[2] That was the aptitude to go with. In quick order, cloth diapers and diaper services went the way of the buggy whip.

Key Tactics of Attribute Positioning
- Tie your word or attribute to key business initiatives or other activities
- Double down on your attribute in all communications so there is a strong link between you and the word
- Use the word consistently at every touchpoint—online and in person
- Lock your attribute in the mind with a memorable phrase, mantra, or battle cry
- Build your leadership philosophy around your attribute

Attribute and Identity Meld

You know you're a brand when one word will do. No one has ever said, "Oprah who?" We're all on a first name basis with the megastar TV interviewer Oprah Winfrey.

In my view, the chief attribute Oprah is aligned with is empathy. It's a strong part of her identity and one of the key reasons for her success as a TV personality and interviewer.

Just watch Oprah interview someone. Her empathy shows in the way she asks questions. In the way she listens. Her empathy gets people to open up like she did in her bombshell interview with the Duke and Duchess of Sussex in 2020. We feel safe sharing our stories with her. We feel she understands us. Not many people can project empathy like Oprah.

Don't Fight What You're Really Good At

Before her breakout role on the sitcom *I Love Lucy*, Lucille Ball was just another struggling actress with a dream of making it big as a movie star. Her career never got beyond landing small parts and modeling gigs.[3] Even her acting teacher told her she'd never be successful.

Though her vision of becoming a movie star fizzled, audiences discovered her true talent, her defining attribute. Lucille Ball was funny. Her differentiator was her exquisite comedic timing and gift for physical comedy. Funny was not an attribute possessed by many actresses, so she stood out.

The Hollywood Model:
Talent + Positioning + Packaging + PR = Star

Once she had the right positioning, a stylist suggested the bright, flaming-red hair color, and Ball pitched her voice higher for her role as Lucy Ricardo. She became America's beloved slapstick queen with the hottest show on network television.[4]

Yet as funny and successful as she was, she always resented being branded as a comedian. She was the best of the best in comedy, but Lucille Ball wanted different positioning. She wanted to be a star on the big screen.

Remember, your brand is how other people see you, and her fans did not see Lucille Ball as glamorous. It was not the right attribute. Funny was. Funny is hard to do, but even harder is repositioning yourself after your brand is established in the minds of others.

Find an Underused Word

Social scientists, experts, researchers, and others often try to coin a different word or a catchphrase to explain their insights or philosophy, and, of course, to grab attention.

The executive coach Brad Stulberg chose the word "groundedness" to define the philosophy behind his consulting practice. He defines it as "the internal strength and self-confidence that sustains you through ups and downs."[5]

Groundedness is not a word people tend to use a lot, so it's more likely to stick in the mind. It's simple, conveys a benefit, and seems particularly appropriate for the new world of work.

5 Attribute Superpowers

1. **Focused on Your Attribute:** The best attributes are simple and convey a benefit that sticks in the mind. The biggest mistake people make is thinking they need to appeal to the entire marketplace or be all things to all people. For brands and for people, it's always smart to narrow the focus to your winning attribute.

2. **Quickly "Click" with Others.** Clicking is a way of instantly connecting and tapping into the social rhythm of other people. Clickers look for similarity and connection with others, often by *subtly and unconsciously imitating* the other person. Try it on your next pitch. Studies show that clickers are likely to get cooperation and a positive response.

3. **Strong Emotional Intelligence (EI):** Emotional intelligence is the ability to pick up subtle emotional clues from others and to tap into your own emotions to communicate successfully, empathize, and mitigate conflict. People with high EI have better mental health, job performance, and leadership skills.

4. **Determined to Get Results:** Attribute positioning is all about focusing on the one attribute that gives you maximum results in terms of career success. If your attribute isn't working as well as in the past, you tweak your brand positioning by changing or evolving your attribute to be relevant in the current marketplace.

5. **Fast Adapter to New Situations:** Most people don't like change, so being quick to adapt to new cultures and environments is a powerful ability. Adaptability is especially important today, where change is predicted to be the new norm.

Exercise: Attribute Personal Brand Statement

Competitive Analysis

- **Identify key competitors:** What attribute they stand for?
- **What attributes are needed?** Can you fill the gap? Why is your attribute more important?

Target Audience

- **Identify who you want to reach:** Be specific, such as your boss, colleagues, customers, etc.
- **What attributes do people associate with you?** Write down your best guess or ask colleagues.
- **What attribute do you want to stand for?** Is it a strength that's needed in your company or line of work?

Sample Positioning Statement

- **Example:** A market researcher decided that the key attribute for her success was her ability to build rapport with women consumers.

Initial sentence: For (marketers, ad agency clients) who need (research on why consumers choose the brands they buy) I stand for (a strong ability to create "rapport" with consumers so they open up about their brand choices)

Final sample positioning statement

Because of my rapport with consumers, my clients call me "The Oprah of Madison Avenue."

Your Attribute Positioning Statement: Select your attribute and use the format below to explore Attribute positioning for Brand You by putting together a draft statement:

Draft Statement: For (target audience) who needs (problem you solve) I stand for (attribute value proposition)

Final Attribute Positioning Statement _____

- **Identify three reasons to believe:** List specific projects and accomplishments, books, articles, papers, awards, and experiences that support your attribute positioning.
- **List three keywords:** Select three adjectives or short keyword phrases that define your attribute.

Attribute Positioning in a Nutshell

Attribute Brand Idea: You stand for an important attribute that sets you apart from others

Keyword: Attribute

Values: Focus, connecting with others, being true to your strengths

Motivation: Strong sense of identity with your attribute

Brand voice: Empathetic

Ideal customers: People who identify with your attribute

Battle cry: Focus on what's important

Chapter 8

Positioning Strategy No. 5 Engineer

D on't think Engineer positioning is just for people out of engineering school. Engineer positioning (also called *Magic Ingredient or New Process* positioning) is for people who reimagine and reengineer things in new ways to solve a problem or create something better.

As an engineer, you are methodical *and* creative. It's a powerful combo. You spot patterns where others see nothing. You like to tinker, experiment, and improve things. You don't like to give up until you've solved the problem. You're a perfectionist who has to ensure that everything is correct before you release findings.

You could be a chef using new food ingredients or secret spices in a novel way or a computer programmer developing a new algorithm that works better than previous programs.

You could create a new way of conducting research that is more accurate or reengineer your company's supply chain. You could be a physical therapist with a different exercise program or a celebrity with a new diet.

The possibilities are endless. Your differentiator is tinkering and improving things. You are creative yet practical.

Are You an Engineer?

Do you like fiddling with objects, ideas, or processes to see if you can make them better?

Did you take things apart when you were a kid to see how they work? Or learn how to cook and create your own recipes as a kid?

Do you like to see how you can make things better for less money?

Are you a critical, methodical thinker who's also creative?

If you answered yes to two or more of these questions, you should consider Strategy 5 Engineer (aka Special Ingredient or New Process positioning).

Engineer Positioning: I developed a special ingredient or a new process _____ that _____

The Engineer Personality

As an engineer, you like to tweak and reengineer things. You're curious and a critical thinker, organized yet highly creative, with good intuition. You're happiest when you're engrossed with a project, caught up in analysis and experimentation to find the best solution to a problem. Even as a child, you loved to tinker and fiddle with everything to make things work better or to create experiments to see what happens.

You are logical, focused, and determined to get results, but you are also creative and like to try new ways of doing things. You have a collaborative spirit and work well with a team or alone. If you like to cook, you often experiment and substitute some of the ingredients or try a different cooking process.

You are fair and reasonable but sometimes can be judgmental. You hold yourself and others to high standards. If things don't meet your expectations, you criticize not only others but also yourself. You can be a perfectionist, because your aim is to improve and perfect things, yourself included.

You tend to be an introvert and more of a loner than a party animal. You have a small circle of friends or colleagues, but you're most content working in depth on a project. You are determined and believe it's important to analyze things thoroughly and never quit until you solve the problem.

Most of the time you:	*But sometimes you:*
■ Prefer in-depth analysis	■ Dislike vague questions
■ Are creative yet methodical	■ Avoid getting too close to others
■ Don't like to quit until you solve a problem	■ Don't like sloppy work

Generally people see you as:	*But you can:*
■ Detail oriented yet creative	■ Avoid commenting until done
■ Thorough and analytical	■ Get bogged down in research
■ A tinkerer who improves things	■ Can avoid people and prefer being alone

If this sounds like you, all the more reason to explore Positioning Strategy No. 5 Engineer.

A Magic Ingredient to Save the World

In the beginning, when Covid-19 was first threatening the world, two vaccine researchers, Uğur Şahin, co-founder and CEO of BioNTech, and Stéphane Bancel, CEO of Moderna, were virtually unknown outside of a small niche of vaccine researchers.

Both had the same quest: to develop a vaccine using mRNA molecules to fight Covid-19. Most of the scientific community were skeptical about their "magic ingredient" and their work on mRNA.[1]

When news of the pandemic broke, in 2020, and its global misery started traveling around the world, both scientists mobilized their teams, working practically around the clock, to find a vaccine. When their vaccine trials came in, Moderna had an efficacy of 94.5 percent, and Pfizer-BioNTech had a 95 percent rate.

The two scientists and their magic ingredient mRNA had hit the ball out of the park.

The Engineering Magic of the Chef

Chefs used to toil outside of the limelight. That is, until chefs starting adopting the Special Process/Magic Ingredient strategy and the celebrity chef was born. Think of Julia Child, Gordon Ramsay, James Beard, Wolfgang Puck, Rachael Ray, and the "Naked Chef," Jamie Oliver. In top restaurants, the chef is often the marquee attraction, not the well-known customers.

Today many celebrity chefs build their brand on television rather than slogging away under a demanding chef in the French tradition. Gordon Ramsay has his feet in both camps. He's a top chef with 16 Michelin stars (and counting) and an intensely competitive, wild-and-crazy chef on television.

Ina Garten started out as an engineer of sorts, analyzing nuclear energy policy at the Office of Management and Budget in Washington, DC.[2]

After her day job, at night she worked her way through Julia Child's recipes in *The Art of French Cooking* (both volumes) for her husband, Jeffrey.

Her culinary activities won out, and she bought a specialty food store in East Hampton, New York, called The Barefoot Contessa, named after a 1945 movie starring Humphrey Bogart and Ava Gardner.

Garten had no formal training as a chef. She built her brand on the Food Network as *"The Barefoot Contessa."* Her "special process" is developing "simple food" that regular folks can master. Her recipes are measured precisely, like a scientific equation, so that they are "fool proof," a skill she no doubt transferred from her budget analyst job. Today, she is one of the most beloved celebrity chefs.

What's Your Secret Sauce?

As an "engineer," you could put new ingredients or components together in a novel way, like Colonel Sanders did with the 11 herbs and spices he used to market KFC, or the secret ingredients in Red Bull that give you an energy boost.

KFC chicken spices are mixed separately in different plants, so not many people know the whole recipe. From a branding perspective, it's hard to know what is more valuable, the recipe or the mystique of a recipe guarded with secret patents. It's the idea that what you don't offer customers is as important as what you do.

Likewise, if you have a secret sauce, it's the one thing people will want to know about you.

The Magic Ingredient That Prevents Cavities

Crest was the first toothpaste to discover fluoride, a "magic" ingredient that reduced cavities.[3] With the American Dental Association "seal of acceptance," Crest launched an advertising campaign featuring children painted by Norman Rockwell, with the headline "Look Mom, No Cavities."

With its magic ingredient, Crest was elevated from cosmetic to therapeutic status and sales skyrocketed. Crest overtook Colgate and has had a multi-decade run as America's favorite toothpaste.[4]

Now almost every brand of toothpaste has fluoride, and we have other oral challenges to worry about, like stains, plaque, bad breath, and sensitive teeth. And there's a host of magic ingredients to fight them.

Crest initially left its formula virtually unchanged until Colgate, with its new ingredients, took the lead. The toothpaste wars continue and now there are hundreds of brands with claims about their ingredients to solve your oral hygiene problems.

A Better Process for Investors

Engineer positioning can be a good strategy for consultants or advisers who have a special approach or process they feel is better than others.

Fueled by evidence that actively managed mutual funds didn't often beat the market, financial executive John Bogle had a different process—"indexing." Instead of having expensive "experts" do the stock picking, why not have a computer mimic a stock index like the S&P 500?

In the early years, Bogle was a very vocal and passionate advocate about indexing's ability to outperform managed funds. He had performance charts to prove it, yet very few investors were interested in his new process. Belief in index funds was so low that the press called them "Bogle's Folly." Now

Bogle's "special process"—indexing—makes up 40 percent of mutual fund investing.[5]

Best Careers for Engineers

This strategy works, of course, for engineers, but also can be a good positioning strategy for consultants, doctors, researchers, scientists, chefs, designers, computer programmers, lawyers, and other professionals—if your value added comes from how you work differently from others. You could be reengineering a process that improves manufacturing costs, or designing a new way to analyze polling statistics that is more accurate.

5 Superpowers of Engineers

1. **Methodical, Process Orientation to Problems:** Perhaps no other positioning strategy is as methodical and process oriented as the Engineer. Engineers use a consistent process that they apply, which includes phases, steps, and procedures to solve a problem.
2. **Experiments to Find Better Solutions:** Engineers are tinkerers who check, recheck, test, and retest to make sure that every detail is correct and nothing falls through the cracks when they are looking for solutions.
3. **Intense Focus on Results:** Engineers create a sense of urgency. They set deadlines and clear and specific goals. Their projects may have many moving parts, but they never take their eye off the ball and their goals.
4. **Exceptional Analytical Skills:** Relevant facts and details are a big deal to the Engineer. They're very organized and their analysis is very thorough. They respond to problems with clear reasoning.
5. **Passionate and Driven:** They're happiest when they are thoroughly immersed in their work, the more challenging the project, the better.

Exercise: Engineer Positioning Statement

Competitive Analysis

- **Identify key competitors:** Define what they stand for.
- **Do you have a special process or magic ingredient?** How does it differentiate you?

Target Audience

- **Identity who you want to reach:** Be specific, such as your boss, colleagues, customers, etc.
- **What problem does your process or special ingredient solve?** What problems exist that you could solve?

Sample Positioning Statement

- **Example:** A computer engineer wanted to position himself as a programmer who solves tough problems.
- **Draft sentence:** For (clients, prospective clients) who need (solutions for tough computer software problems) I stand for (a programmer who doesn't give up).

Final sample positioning statement:

The patient, persistent programmer who solves tough problems.

Your Engineer (Special Process) Positioning Statement: Use the format below to explore Engineer positioning for Brand You by putting together a draft statement:

Draft Statement: For (target audience) who needs (problem you solve) I stand for (value proposition)

Final Engineer Positioning Statement _____

- **Identify three reasons to believe:** List projects and accomplishments, books, articles, papers, awards, and experiences that support positioning yourself as an engineer who has a special process, magic ingredient, or successful way of working.

- **List three keywords:** Select three adjectives or short keyword phrases that define you as an engineer.

Engineer Positioning in a Nutshell

Engineer Brand Idea: You have developed a different process or special ingredient that has improved something

Keywords: Special process, magic ingredient, engineer

Values: Focus, making things more efficient or better

Motivation: Strong desire to improve things

Brand voice: Analytical and creative

Ideas customers: People who appreciate your method

Battle cry: Everything can be improved

Chapter 9

Positioning Strategy No. 6 Expert

B eing a jack-of-all-trades, a generalist who knows a little about a lot of things, is not a smart personal brand strategy. What is smart is to be an expert in one, clearly defined area. A specialist with a fresh message sends out a strong signal and breaks through the noise.

Focus is powerful. The key ingredient of the expert strategy is in-depth knowledge of a specific area. *The narrower the focus, the more powerful the brand*, is generally the rule in branding. We are in an era in which specialists thrive and generalists do not. That's why experts are valued and tend to be paid more.

In executing the *expert strategy*, it helps to be able to interpret something in a new way or to have your own philosophy and standards. You can put ideas together in a meaningful way or explain the fine points of complicated subjects, even minutiae, so that everyone understands.

A smart way to go is to choose an area that is not crowded with experts, so that you can stand out. Or you could find an arena where the current experts are not doing a good job of communicating. Or you could focus on a niche where you can stand out with your in-depth knowledge.

Another tactic is to be the contrary voice. Industry conferences and media like to have a contrarian expert who goes against the grain to add balance, a different point of view, and a little excitement to the discussion.

Are You an Expert?

Do you know one thing really well? Or plan to in the future?

Is there an area you are passionate about that could be the focus of your expertise?

Are you recognized as a thought leader in your arena?

Is there a niche that lacks experts, where you can stand out?

Can you identify areas where you've made a contribution as an expert?

If you've answered yes to two or more of these questions, consider Positioning Strategy No. 6 Expert.

Expert Positioning: I am an expert in _____

The Expert Personality

Experts are focused, hardworking, and conscientious. You're a hedgehog who knows one thing really well. You have in-depth knowledge, expertise, and strong credentials in your area of expertise. Your special topic is your passion, and you stay in touch with new developments in your area of expertise.

You are goal oriented, determined, and well organized. Your goal is to make an important contribution to your field as an expert. If you decide to explore something, you test and retest. You will go all the way to the end to accomplish your goals.

You make deliberate decisions based on intense research and analysis. You think carefully before you speak and impress others with your understanding of a subject. Because of your knowledge, you are highly trusted by others, and the trust of others is important to you.

You are stable, steady, and dependable, even in chaotic times. People know they can count on you. Reliability is part of your DNA.

Most of the time you:	But sometimes you:
■ Focus on a topic in depth ■ Do more than what is expected ■ Stay up-to-date on your specialty	■ Drive the team too hard ■ Lose patience with sloppy people ■ Can be too narrowly focused

Generally people see you as:	But you can:
■ Knowledgeable, analytical ■ Deliberate, careful, thoughtful ■ Hard-working and trustworthy	■ Rely too much on tradition ■ Be overly analytical and miss the big picture ■ Be unyielding about working until the job is done

If this sounds like you, all the more reason to explore Positioning Strategy No. 6 Expert.

Experts Know One Big Thing

A lot of infectious disease experts popped into our consciousness throughout the Covid-19 pandemic and afterward.

One expert stands out—Doctor Anthony Fauci. With his direct, data-driven approach, Dr. Fauci became the embodiment of the public health effort in the United States.

In the early days of Covid-19, when Americans were scared and didn't know much about coronaviruses, Dr. Fauci provided information in easy-to-understand language in daily television appearances from the White House, leading to the nickname "the explainer-in-chief of the coronavirus epidemic."[1]

Then, on March 23, 2020, Dr. Fauci didn't appear at President Trump's daily briefing in the White House press room.

Twitter went crazy. #NoFauci began trending.

People were worried. He wasn't just any expert, he was a trustworthy expert that people relied on. Who will be candid about what's going on if we lose Dr. Fauci? Things were tense until the White House put him back on the air on a daily basis.

Expert Credentials

With impeccable credentials in infectious disease, there's no doubt that Dr. Fauci is an expert. He has had a lifelong focus on one big thing—infectious disease. He graduated first in his class at Cornell University Medical College. He directed the National Institute of Allergy and Infectious Diseases through six administrations.

Most important, he was a trusted expert at the epicenter of many viral epidemics: HIV, SARS, avian influenza, swine flu, Zika, Ebola, and others. Now he's one of the most well-known experts in the United States.

Every organization, every industry, every person needs experts. Companies like H&R Block, in taxes, and McKinsey, with its army of industry and functional experts, use the expert strategy to position their companies.

Consider carving out a niche that you can be the expert in. Remember, the media and industry leaders are always looking for a new face, for someone who will interpret something in a fresh way or who has a different point of view.

Pounce on an Information Gap

You may admire Barbara Corcoran as a savvy celebrity investor on the TV show *Shark Tank*. But I admire how she used the expert strategy to propel herself into the stratosphere in the New York City real estate community, early in her career.

After cycling through twenty different jobs in her twenties, she found her calling selling residential real estate in New York City. In the mid-1970s and 1980s, high-end real estate was pretty much ruled by what I and others like to refer to as "ladies in mink with keys to the best apartments."

Corcoran didn't come from money. She was one of ten children from a working-class, Irish Catholic family in New Jersey. Corcoran didn't go for a fur coat, but she did invest in a designer coat from Bergdorf's that she bought with her first commission check.

With just one year of experience and a dozen real estate sales to her name, Corcoran saw the white space, a gap in the market. There was very little reliable information on the sales prices of high-end residential real estate in Manhattan at that time. The ladies in mink kept sales prices very hush-hush.

Corcoran decided to break through the embargo on information.

Share Your "Expert" Info

The expert strategy is perfectly suited for visibility tactics like media interviews, bylined columns, social media posts, online courses, newsletters, and podcasts.

After her first year in real estate, Corcoran created a real estate report called the *Corcoran Report,* which revealed the average sales price of luxury apartments in Manhattan based on the dozen apartments her company had sold. Corcoran made sixty copies and sent it to every reporter at the *New York Times.*

Formerly a nobody, Corcoran became *the* real estate expert in New York City when she and her report landed on the front page of the Sunday *New York Times* real estate section.

Skip the 10,000 Hours

Let's analyze this. Corcoran was hardly an "expert" at the time, with her limited real estate experience of about a year. Forget the 10,000 hours of practice needed to become an expert, featured in Malcolm Gladwell's book *Outliers* (now debunked in other studies).[2]

Corcoran leapfrogged the competition and became the queen of New York real estate through her own moxie. The so-called experts kept their real estate expertise wrapped in mystery.

She preempted the expert role; the media is always looking for experts and "secret" information, and Corcoran was glad to oblige.

Seek Third-Party Endorsements

There's nothing like the value of a prominent person or celebrity endorsing your expertise. Corcoran excelled in that tactic as well.

For another edition of the *Corcoran Report*, Corcoran decided to focus on the most expensive apartments in the world. It was 1983, and Donald Trump was building Trump Tower, which he was branding as the "most expensive condominium in the world."

Corcoran wanted to interview Donald Trump but got turned down. She told the secretary to tell Mr. Trump that according to her analysis, Trump Tower was not the most expensive but was near the bottom of her top ten list of the world's most expensive apartments.[3]

As you can imagine, she got in to see Mr. Trump pretty quickly with that message. Trump convinced her that Trump Tower was the most expensive and he agreed to include the Corcoran Group branding with its most expensive claim in all his advertising. Barbara Corcoran's brand as the expert in high-end New York City apartments was sealed.

After selling her company, she's done a rebrand as a media personality and expert on entrepreneurship on *Shark Tank*.

A Different Point of View

Branded "The Oracle of Omaha," Warren Buffett is one of the wealthiest, most successful, and most influential investors in the world.

He's totally self-made. Born in Nebraska, he bought his first stock at 11 years old. After getting turned down at Harvard Business School, he ended up at Columbia Business School. Turns out it was a lucky break, because he studied with the two creators of value investing, Benjamin Graham and David Dodd. Buffett found his calling.

Buffett became the most famous and respected promoter of value investing, an investing style based on buying stocks that are inexpensive in relation to their sales, earnings, and assets so they offer good value.

In other words, he ignores the hot stocks that dominate the news and looks for cheap stocks with high dividends that many investors ignore. And he has a battle cry for investors that explains his investment philosophy: "It's far better to buy a wonderful stock at a fair price than a fair company at a wonderful price."[4]

Buffett has beaten the market, year after year, by sticking to his principles of investing in "businesses," not "stocks."

Popularize Your Topic

Today Buffett is a god among value investors, and his annual letter is their bible. For over 40 years, Buffett has written an open letter to investors in his company, Berkshire Hathaway. It's a must-read across the investing world because of his track record and his ability to explain complicated subjects simply.

So what's Buffett's secret for communicating in clear talk for complicated topics? He's told reporters that he writes each letter as if he's writing to his two sisters. "It's 'Dear Doris and Bertie' at the start and then I take that off at the end."

Experts = Trusted Source

Getting visibility is important for brands and for you, too. Brands with high visibility tend to dominate the market and get a higher price. Gaining visibility as an expert can add value to your career and how you're perceived by others, too.

People have trust in experts because they have credentials that demonstrate they know one thing really well. It could be education and degrees, job experience, projects, awards, research, certifications, achievements, apprenticeships, papers and books, mentorships, and media recognition.

The pandemic propelled dozens of new medical experts into the spotlight—doctors, nurses, hospital administrators, medical professors, public health professionals. Working from home spiked demand for experts in home improvement, remote working, and cooking.

Who knows what experts will be in demand next year? Or next month? Some experts are in demand all the time, like stock market experts, economists, politicians, and others. As an expert you'll need to figure out how you fit in and be adept at keeping your talking points up to date.

The book route is another way to go. If you've written a book on a topic, you are immediately perceived as an expert. How could you have written a book, unless you are an expert?

Best Careers for Experts

Consider carving out a niche that you can be the expert in. Remember, the media is always looking for a new face, for someone who will interpret something in an easily understandable way or has a different point of view.

The expert strategy is perfect for many professionals such as accountants, financial advisers, lawyers, product experts, and the like. If you're a consultant who handles every type of client, you will have a lot of competition. But if you have a specialty, people will likely be willing to pay a premium for expert advice. You can be the accountant who specializes in the legal community. Lawyers will pay a premium for your advice because you understand their business.

You could implement the expert strategy if you're in an expert role at a large company. One colleague in a financial services company was an expert in retirement plans and, importantly, also an expert in the Employee Retirement Income Security Act of 1974 (ERISA). She got certified and stays up to date. No one in her company understands its compliance rules as well as she does, making her the go-to person and giving her job security.

5 Superpowers of Experts

1. **Knows One Thing Very Well:** The genius is to figure out the one big thing that is a passion, where you can excel and stand out from others, so that when people think of you they think of your expert area.
2. **In-Depth Thinker and Thought Leader:** Experts are analytical thinkers who like to dig deep into one topic where they can be recognized as a leading voice and commentator.
3. **Outstanding Credentials:** The credibility of an expert is very important, so credentials are key: academic, educational, publications,

industry awards, and the like. An exception is an influencer expert more likely to build expertise through self-taught or unconventional means.

4. **Excellent Communicator and Explainer:** Experts who are media- and career savvy have a knack for communicating complex information simply or making it fascinating.

5. **Strong PR Platform for Expertise:** Experts are often sought by the media and industry conferences to shed light on their area of expertise. The best experts have outstanding communication skills and engagement with their audience.

Exercise: Expert Personal Brand Statement

Competitive Analysis

- **Identify and analyze two or three experts:** In your industry, company, or selected arena
- **What sets you apart as an expert?** Write down your thoughts.

Target Audience

- **Identify who you want to reach:** Be specific, such as your boss, colleagues, customers, job search contacts, industry leaders, the media, etc.
- **Define the problem your expertise solves for them:** Write down your thoughts.

Sample Positioning Statement

Example: An investment professional wanted to be recognized as a digital assets expert, a newer frontier in investing.

Draft Sentence: For investors, financial media who need expert investment advice on new asset classes I stand for insight into digital assets

Final Sample Positioning Statement:

Digital Assets Expert—the Next Wave of Investing

Your Expert Positioning Statement: Use the format below to explore expert positioning for Brand You by putting together a draft statement:

Draft Statement: For (<u>target audience</u>) who needs (<u>problem you solve</u>) I stand for (<u>value proposition</u>)

Final Expert Positioning Statement _____

- **Identify three reasons to believe:** List everything you've done that supports your expert positioning such as jobs, research, intellectual property, media interviews, white papers, website, bylined articles, courses, and the like.
- **List three keywords:** That define your expertise

The Expert Brand in a Nutshell

Expert Brand Idea: In-depth knowledge and trusted source in area of expertise

Keyword: Expert in _____

Values: Intellect, data, insightful point of view

Motivation: Communicating your knowledge to help others

Brand voice: Thoughtful, authoritative, knowledgeable

Ideal customers: People or companies who want an expert opinion

Battle cry: Know one thing really well.

Chapter 10

Positioning Strategy
No. 7 Target Market

W̶ho would you choose? A professional who works with a wide range of clients? Or one whose entire practice is limited to people just like you? It's an easy question for most of us to answer.

That's why Target Market (also called *User*) positioning can be so powerful. You don't try to appeal to everyman but to a specific target group of customers, to their quirks, preferences, lifestyle, needs, and attitude.

In short, target market positioning is not about you; it's about your users.

A classic example of target market positioning in the branding world is the "Pepsi Generation" campaign launched in the early 1960s just as baby boomers and youth culture were taking over.

Pepsi did something revolutionary, something that was completely different from what brands did in those days. It focused on the attributes of people who drink Pepsi rather than the attributes of the product.

Pepsi's marketing was all about young people having fun and doing active things like playing volleyball on the beach. Young people loved the campaign and its focus on their lifestyle. Sales took off.

This is a great positioning strategy for professionals who only handle a certain type of client. You create a community through your understanding of their needs, desires, and point of view, and they reward you with loyalty. In many ways, you know your target audience better than anyone else, even better than they know themselves.

Is Target Market Positioning Right for You?

Do you have an affinity or connection with a specific group of people that you understand and can serve better than others?

Do you see unique opportunities for building your career or launching a new product around your knowledge of a particular group?

Do you have a strong customer service orientation?

Are there aspects of your background, credentials, or experience that would make you a perfect fit for a specific target audience?

Is there a target group that you feel you can help better than others?

If you answered yes to two or more of these questions, then you may want to position yourself using Strategy No. 8 Target Market Positioning.

Target Market Positioning: The target group I identify with is _____because_____

The Target Market Personality

Everyone says they are customer oriented, but you really are. Your goal is to build your professional brand around a core group of customers who you connect with emotionally and intellectually through shared values, lifestyle, and point of view.

You not only understand your target audience, you connect with them deeply. You identify with them and feel empathy toward them. They are your special community—your tribe—and your aim is to know them better and solve their needs better than anyone else. You understand their aspirations, attitudes, and psychological makeup. In return, your tribe trusts that you have their interests foremost in your mind, and you do.

You are a good listener and highly attentive and considerate toward your clients. You understand their problems and go to great lengths to help solve them, but you do understand boundaries and know how to react appropriately.

The key ingredient of the target market positioning mindset is a clear-cut, laser focus on your target audience, not yourself. It's a perfect match. You seek out like-minded people and identify with them, and they identify with and highly recommend you.

Most of the time you:	*But sometimes you:*
■ Self-identify with a group	■ Can lose sight of the big
■ Are patient and considerate	picture
■ Have new ideas that will	■ Avoid conflicts
delight your users	■ Get numb instead of angry

Generally people see you as:	*But you can:*
■ Very attentive to needs of	■ Sacrifice your needs for others
others	■ Not express your desires
■ A good listener	■ Steer clear of confrontations
■ Good at helping others	and disagreements

If this personality profile sounds like you, all the more reason to explore Positioning Strategy No. 7 Target Market.

A Shared Lifestyle and Point of View

Whether you are a part of biker culture and go to the annual roundup in Sturgis, South Dakota, or are more of a weekend rider, you know Harley-Davidson.

Hogs are big, fast, and American.

Harley isn't selling a bike as much as a way of life, a counterculture of freedom. You're making a statement about who you are when you ride a Harley, and its tagline says it all: "Screw it, let's ride."

Unlike most beverages that go the expensive, blockbuster TV commercial route, Red Bull went rogue. Its marketing didn't focus on the product, it was aimed directly at its target audience: 18- to 35-year-old men.

Red Bull's marketing has always been about its customers with content and experiences young people crave, like extreme sporting events. Its tagline is "Red Bull gives you wings," the energy you need to live your hyper-active lifestyle.

What Would Excite Your Base?

Starbucks is also focused on its customers: urban, affluent, and busy professionals looking to get their daily caffeine fix. The Starbucks mission is to create the best customer experience, starting with writing your name on each cup when you order and letting customers tailor drinks to suit their taste.

It's become a game for some Starbucks fans to try to outdo each other on social media, like TikTok, by posting elaborate concoctions as "Starbucks Secret Menu." One influencer who posts as "Annalovescoffee" shared her creation: "a Venti cold brew with caramel syrup and vanilla sweet cream cold foam, apple brown sugar syrup, apple in the foam and cinnamon dolce on top."[1]

Like Attracts Like

Finding your customer niche is easier than you think. Begin with who you are and what you already know best. Reflect on your passions, interests, and experiences. Is there a demographic or psychographic group you're a part of where it would be relatively easy for you to make the focus of your business or job?

You could be the accountant or business consultant who handles only entrepreneurs. Or the career coach who just works with corporate employees who want to transition to a more meaningful career. Or the financial consultant whose business targets retirees or women or succession planning for family businesses.

Once you find your niche, the key to executing the target market strategy is to do a mind meld with your users. You want to build a very powerful connection—a shared identity—with your tribe. It's a winning positioning, particularly with consultants, coaches, financial advisers, lawyers, customer advocates, and influencers, because you create a community with your customers and their needs, desires, and points of view.

Think of it as a community of kindred spirits. You understand your target market emotionally at their core, with who they are as people. You know what they need, the problems they have, what makes them tick. They are your preferred customers and they prefer you and your products and services.

Customer Persona Creation

You may think you know your target audience well, but to come up with new ideas to align with their needs, frustrations, and goals, it helps to draw up a *customer avatar* or *customer persona* like marketers do. It's a fictional archetype that describes and captures your target audience.

Here's one way to do it. Outline the key traits that define your target audience: personal information like average age, marital status, their interests, and worries. Write a description about what a day in the life looks like. What frustrates this person? What is their career story?

Rather than just answer these questions in your mind, write it up as a fictional customer profile with a name, picture, and short descriptions: lifestyle, a day in the life, personal details (age, marital status), challenges, and sources for news and information.

Once you have your customer profile clear in your mind, how to market yourself to them becomes clear.

Who Are You Going to Call?

When you stand for a certain type of client, people who fit that profile will come your way. People have a reason to call you, because you have a lot of experience with people just like them. You are familiar with their problems and desires.

If you're a woman victim of sexual harassment, who are you going to seek for your legal counsel?

Women's rights attorney Gloria Allred, of course.

Client Niche = PR Platform

Over four decades, long before #MeToo or #TimesUp, Allred's special niche has been women who have been victimized. A former schoolteacher, she has a reputation for representing women against high-profile men.

She's a recognized master of managing the media narrative around her cases. And she has an impressive track record of winning.

Her specialty has given her media attention unmatched by most of her competitors and made her a legal celebrity as well.

Bonding Through a Shared History

So why did Allred base her legal career and law firm on victims? She identifies with women victims because she was one herself.

In the Netflix documentary *Talking Allred*, she shares the story of her rape. "It's always personal to me if a woman is a victim of injustice. My commitment to women comes from my own life."[2]

Focusing on a specific market niche has been a winning personal brand strategy for Allred. On her website she brands herself as "the most famous woman attorney practicing law in the nation today" and as a "fearless lawyer, feminist, activist, television and radio commentator" who is "fighting on the front lines for victim's rights."[3]

The Power of the Influencer

A modern way to adopt target market positioning is to be an influencer with an engaged online community of people who share your passions. Many influencers often start out with a niche in technology, health, travel, or beauty and build their target market from that foundation.

An Influencer's power comes from
influencing the buying decisions of followers

It may look easy, but being an influencer is a semi- or full-time job. You've got to continuously make content, respond to fans, and come up with ideas to stand out from others. Getting engaging pictures and frequently refreshing them takes time. Everything in your daily life needs to be recorded and shared on the internet.

An influencer's personality is a big part of the draw, but they've got to continually stoke the fire so fans are active and engaged with a lot of back and forth commentary. Or your community will look elsewhere.

When an influencer has a large group of highly engaged fans, amazing things can happen. Maybe you won't end up as a top influencer on Instagram like Kylie Jenner and Christiano Ronaldo, with millions of dedicated followers and who are paid top dollar for posts by brands. But you're likely to be rewarded with product endorsements and advertising revenue just the same, if you have over 1,000-plus avid fans in your community.

Your association counts, too. Over 90 percent of consumers trust what influencers say, over traditional advertising, according to Nielsen's Consumer Trust Index.[4]

5 Superpowers of Target Market Positioning

1. **Shared Identity with a Target Audience:** You make your tribe feel important and you're rewarded with their loyalty. You have a community, a shared identity with others who share a similar culture, values, activities, desires, and points of view.

2. **Strong Customer Focus and Customer Service Orientation:** You go the extra mile for your "customers." If you're an employee in an organization, your "customers" are your boss, senior managers, colleagues, and clients. If you are a professional running your own business, your clients are your customers. Whichever camp your customers are in, you treat them like gold.

3. **In-Depth Knowledge of the Target Group:** Great things can happen with a narrow focus on a target group. You know a lot about your target group: how they think, what's different about them compared to other demographic and psychographic groups. Your knowledge is valuable, in terms of intellectual property, PR, industry recognition, compensation, and product development.

4. **Strong Referral Business:** Nothing beats good word of mouth, and you know how to get people talking. Because you prioritize your target audience demographic, they actively promote you to others, and you reward them for their referrals.

5. **Trusted Partner:** Because you and your community have a shared purpose, a common cause that is the "why" behind your actions, you are highly trusted by your target audience.

Target Marketing Positioning Brand Statement

Competitive Analysis

- **Identify and analyze competitors focused on the same niche:** In your industry, company, or selected arena
- **How are you different from your competitors?** Write down your thoughts on how your relationship with your target audience niche is special.

Target Audience

- **Define your target audience:** Be specific, such as your boss, colleagues, customers, job search contacts, industry leaders, the media, etc.
- **What problem do you solve for your target audience?** Write down your thoughts.

Sample Target Market Positioning Statement

Example: A business consultant wanted to focus on entrepreneurs who wanted to grow their business to the next level.

Initial Positioning Sentence: For <u>entrepreneurs </u>who need <u>a growth strategy</u> I stand for<u> strategies and tactics to build your new venture into a big brand</u>

Final Sample Positioning Sentence:

The Small Business Advocate: Growing a Small Business into a Big Brand

Your Target Market Positioning Statement: Use the format below to define your special user niche and explore Target Marketing positioning for Brand You.

For (<u>target audience</u>) who needs (<u>problem you solve</u>) I stand for (<u>value proposition</u>)

Final Target Market Positioning Statement _____

- **Identify three reasons to believe:** Give three examples of experience, knowledge, background, and events that demonstrate your target market connection.
- **List three keywords:** Select three adjectives or short keyword phrases that define your Target Market positioning.

Target Market Positioning in a Nutshell

Target Brand Idea: Shared identity with a specific target community

Keyword: Target group

Values: Community, identity with target group

Motivation: Connecting with and helping specific target audience

Brand voice: Caring, knowledgeable

Ideal customers: People or companies who want to be part of a coherent community of compatible people

Battle cry: A community of like-minded people is powerful.

Chapter 11

Positioning Strategy No. 8 Elite

Elite or luxury brands are superior in every way: excellent quality, expensive, and often hard to get. Spendy brands communicate elevated status and have *pricing power*. They can increase the price and still maintain demand. You want to have pricing power, too, or people will think of you as the bargain brand.

In fact, high price is a key reason elite brands are appealing to their customer base. First, it shows you can afford them, and for many people, high price signals superiority. It seems obvious that a $1,000-an-hour consultant must be better than a $200-an-hour consultant (or lawyer, or any other role). They can cite their stellar background and superior track record of accomplishments to justify a top salary or high fees.

Being hard to get and creating faux scarcity are often a compelling part of this brand strategy. Look at the way luxury-goods manufacturers produce a very limited run of the hot new item so it sells out within minutes and has a waiting list. Scarcity creates a sales frenzy of desire and gives brands the mystique of the elite.

The elite strategy can be a tough act to pull off in personal branding.

You're either elite or you're not. Are you in the top ten percent in your industry? Or part of the governing elite? The A List? Or the arts elite? The One Percent?

You've got to project yourself as someone who's elite, who has connections, and who knows what they're worth.

But if you are an elite, it's a powerful advantage. In many ways, our society is moving from a meritocracy to a celebritocracy, and you're one of the lucky ones who can take advantage of its benefits.

Are You an Elite—Excellent, Expensive, and Worth It?

Do you have a superior track record that justifies a top job and top salary?
Is there a lot of demand for what you do and a scarcity of qualified people?
Do you have the confidence to pull off a high-price strategy?
Are you among the top tier in your line of work?
Are you well connected with outstanding contacts?

If you answered yes to two or more of these questions, then you may want to position yourself using Positioning Strategy No. 8 Elite.

> **Elite Positioning: I am an elite and in the top tier because** _____

The Elite Personality

As a top-tier player in your profession or designated arena, you value your worth. You don't do "adequate." You're confident in your superior ability. You have a well-deserved reputation in your field as top class. There's no doubt in your mind that your knowledge, talent, and abilities put you in the top tier, and you want others to recognize your value.

You've never been accused of having imposter syndrome. You have high self-esteem and self-confidence. In your estimation, you have superior abilities compared to your competitors that put you in the top ten percent. Or the top one percent. You're ambitious and determined, and you know people. You're proud of your achievements and are well paid. In your mind, you earned it and are worth every penny.

Sometimes you feel superior to others or feel that you deserve the best things in life. You like luxury and buy only the top quality in everything to maintain a high standard of living. You often need to feel important and recognized as an achiever.

You like to see yourself as special, hard to get, and in demand and want others to see you that way too. Sometimes you create the illusion that you're more in a demand than is the case, to bolster your top-tier image. You have a well-appointed office and like to create a personalized, upscale experience for your clients and colleagues. After all, you believe in keeping up appearances, and while some of your indulgences may be gratuitous luxuries, you want them all the same. Your clothing, cars, houses, and lifestyle are an extension of your elite status.

Most of the time you:

- Have high self-esteem and confidence
- Are recognized as a leader
- Enjoy a high-quality lifestyle

But sometimes you:

- Overindulge yourself
- Can be materialistic
- Appear more successful than you are

Generally people see you as:

- Successful and confident
- Doing what you please
- Interested in your social class

But you can:

- Focus on appearances
- Feel superior to others
- Be arrogant or cold

If this sounds like you, you should consider Strategy No. 8 Elite positioning.

The One Percenter with the $625 Baseball Cap

The baseball-style cap worn by Logan and Kendall Roy in the hit HBO show *Succession* appears ordinary, but it's fueling a buying frenzy among the well-to-do in the United States.[1] The cap doesn't even appear to have a logo. As some have pointed out, if you have a high-def television you might observe the cashmere texture.

The appeal of the cap is that it is so elite that only savvy One Percenters can even recognize that it's no ordinary baseball cap. It is a $625 cap made with luxurious baby cashmere by the elite Italian brand Loro Piana, owned by luxury brand LVMH. The cap is a coded signifier of affluence.

As a company, Loro Piana uses elite positioning and focuses on clothes made from the finest, scarcest, most expensive fabrics in the world. They discovered a rare fiber, "baby cashmere," made from the fleece of infant hircus goats found in northern China and Mongolia.

Baby cashmere can only be harvested once, when the kids are between three and 12 months old, and each one produces only 35 grams of fiber. Some Loro Piana cashmere baseball caps go for over $1,000. Now that's exclusivity and elitism.

Does High Price = Superiority?

When something is expensive, most of us think it is better than something that is cheaper. Look at the wine tasting in which volunteers were asked to evaluate five wines. Each bottle was labeled according to its price: $5, $10, $35, $45, and $90.[2]

Naturally, everyone liked the expensive wines best. But they were all tricked. The most expensive wine, at $90 (its actual retail price), was also presented as a cheap $10 wine, and the $5 wine was also behind the $45 label.

Brain scans were done as the tasters sipped the wine, and it turns out their brains were fooled too! Brains registered more pleasure when people thought they were drinking expensive wine. The test was done later with no price information, and the wine testers rated the cheapest wine as the best. Other wine tests done in Europe and the United States had similar results.

Turns out, wine tasting is a very subjective experience greatly influenced by price. Most people can't taste a difference between elite, expensive wines and cheap, house wines. They just assume when something's expensive, it must be better.

Scarcity Fuels FOMO (Fear of Missing Out)

Marketers have long known that scarcity fuels a brand's value, awareness, and desirability.

Getting something that is hard to get makes people feel lucky that they were able to get it while others lost out, whether it's the "hot" toy for your kids or the Maybach Edition 100. (And maybe they feel a smidge of schadenfreude toward those left out.)

If a brand was available to everyone in the quantity they desired, it wouldn't be very elitist, would it?

Abracadabra

Partnering with a celebrity has long been part of the elite branding tool kit. Look at Yeezy Gap, the fashion venture between Ye (formerly Kanye West) and the Gap.

When the first jackets and hoodies dropped, on September 29, 2021, they sold out in minutes, achieving the biggest single-day sale for any Gap item ever.[3]

Now Yeezy Gap is going more elite, with a partnership with French fashion house Balenciaga in a new collection dubbed Yeezy Gap Engineered by Balenciaga.

You may want to cultivate partnerships with a "celebrity" or two yourself—celebrities in the sense they are well-known people in your line of work. Celebrity connections will throw a little magic dust on how people see you.

Are You an Elite?

The elite are not your everyday top performers. Be realistic. Don't let your hubris run away with you. Elite status is not that common. You've got to be among the best of the best and be connected with the best of the best.

We think in terms of the "Washington elite" in government, the business elite on Wall Street, the "A List" in Hollywood, and so on. One way of understanding the world is to recognize top performers and create a hierarchy within groups and elites.

Money has always been a part of elite ranking. Elite brands are high quality *and* expensive. And high price, in and of itself, gives a brand or a person the perception of being elite, as we observed in the wine tasting test. The CEO who is paid $20 million must be better than the one who is paid $1 million or a mere $200,000. "They must be worth more or how else could they be paid that much?" is how the thinking goes.

Often, having celebrity clients or friends can help you position yourself as a member of the elite. Sometimes, a high profile alone is enough to justify elite status.

Staying Elite

Many former government officials cash in when they enter the private sector because of their elite government contacts and knowledge of how things get done.

If you use this strategy, you've got to have the confidence and financial ability to push away some desirable opportunities if the price or the client isn't right.

Otherwise, you won't convey the impression that you are hard to get, expensive, and worth it. You also want to continuing burnishing your elite credentials by new assignments, positions, and accomplishments.

Above all, you want to convey exclusivity. You may only accept new clients through referrals. Or maybe appointments are hard to get.

Play a Little Hard to Get

You can create a sense of scarcity too, by having options and playing it cool when you get a call about a job or setting up a meeting. If the recruiter asks for an interview, don't agree to come by or do a Zoom call the same day.

That's not an elite move. Plus, it will position you as someone who's easy to get.

The key in the interview process is to be interested in an appropriate-but-not-too-eager level to signal that you are selective and have to do your due diligence. You don't want to come across as difficult, but as someone who knows your worth and who is by no means desperate.

An Elite Brand Experience

With an elite brand, the design, packaging, and shopping experience are just as important as the quality and exclusivity of the brand.

Everything must communicate quality and specialness. For elite services, too, it's about creating a unique and memorable experience every time. It's about knowing what your elite customers like, and giving it to them.

You could create a special office environment by displaying diplomas, prizes, and awards on the walls of your office or in your background on Zoom calls. Or you could have a top-flight interior designer create a jaw-dropping office space. It could be gestures like making it a point to provide a chauffeured car to pick up a client for lunch at a hard-to-get-into restaurant.

You want everything to scream "elite."

Five Superpowers of Elites

1. **Perceived as Best in Class:** People who brand themselves with Elite positioning are confident, top quality, and ambitious. They have strong credentials, a high profile, and an impeccable image.

2. **Rolodex of Elite Contacts:** Elites know other elites: in business, government, the arts. They are likely to know everyone who's somebody, and then some. They are sought out by a lot of people because of their elite status and connections.

3. **Busy, in Demand, and Hard to Get:** Elites like to play off the scarcity principle and create the perception that they are happy where they are. They are highly confident in their abilities, and would need a high offer to pique interest. They tend to be active in various arenas where they are viewed as a power player.

4. **Well Dressed and Well Appointed:** Elites know that image and visuals speak loudly and use them to reiterate their positioning as elite, expensive, and top quality. They tend to be impeccably dressed with expensive, quality clothes and a powerful personal presence.

5. **Superior to Most People:** Elites can feel a sense of entitlement or superiority to others who do what they do. They have an unswerving belief that they are the best (and they just might be).

Exercise: Elite Personal Brand Statement

Competitive Analysis

- **Identify two or three top-tier people:** In your competitive set, select one or two that you feel represent an elite positioning
- **What gives you elite status?** Write down your thoughts.

Target Audience

- **Identify who you want to reach:** Be specific, such as your boss, colleagues, customers, etc. Visualize their identity, personality, values, and lifestyle.
- **What advantage will elite status provide?** Write down your thoughts.

Sample Positioning Statement

Example: A preeminent trial lawyer wanted to position himself among the elite trial lawyers who have achieved precedent-setting results.

Initial sentence: For (legal community, media, prospective clients) who need (a top trial lawyer) I stand for (trial lawyer who is among the legal elite who won a precedent-setting settlement)

Final Sample Positioning Sentence:

Award-Winning Lawyer: Ranked in the Top Ten Lawyers of the Year

Your Elite Positioning Statement: Use the format below to explore Elite positioning for Brand You by putting together a draft statement.

Draft Statement: For (target audience) who needs (problem you solve) I stand for (elite value proposition)

Final Elite Positioning Statement _____

- **Identify three reasons to believe:** List proof of elite credentials, experience, projects, accomplishments, books, articles, papers, awards, and connections that support positioning yourself as an elite.

- **List three keywords:** Select three adjectives or short keyword phrases that define you as an elite.

The Elite Brand in a Nutshell

Elite Brand Idea: You are an elite: talented, hard to get, and worth it

Values: Knowledge and appreciation of the best quality

Motivation: Strong desire to stand out because of your superior knowledge and ability

Brand voice: Confident, sophisticated

Ideal customers: People who feel higher priced means more value

Battle cry: It always pays to go for the best.

Chapter 12

Positioning Strategy No. 9 Heritage

Heritage is valuable as a positioning strategy because it's a unique advantage that others—your competitors—aren't likely to match. With so many people competing for similar goals, having a special heritage and history is a powerful way to stand out and build trust.

Being heir to a certain heritage or country of origin can be a strong selling point for a brand. Think of Swiss watches, Belgian chocolates, Scotch whiskey, and Persian carpets.

Country of origin isn't the only way to claim a special heritage. If your last name is Kennedy, Vanderbilt, Rockefeller, or Bush, you have not only the money, you have a special family heritage that can give you acclaim, visibility, and leverage. And it's a legacy that can be passed down from generation to generation.

Top organizations attract the best people. At least that's the mythology. So your special heritage can be prestigious schools that you attended. The pedigree of the Ivy League always impresses.

Maybe you've done a stint at a well-known company or had an apprenticeship in a prestigious training program. An important award or recognition can put you in the heritage camp. If you're a chef, maybe you studied at Le Cordon Bleu or apprenticed at a multiple-Michelin-starred restaurant.

Do You Have a Special Heritage?

Do you have special heritage that you can leverage from your background?

Does your work experience—companies, training programs—stand out from others?

Is your education impressive or unusual?

Do you have special awards or certifications that give you a unique heritage?

Does your country of origin or languages you speak give you a special heritage?

If you answered yes to two or more of these questions, then you may want to position yourself using Strategy No. 9 Heritage positioning.

> **Heritage Positioning: I offer an advantage because of my special heritage, _____**

The Heritage Personality

You see your inheritance as something that has great value, and you have a strong sense of identity connected to your special history. You are good at tapping into the positive advantages of your background.

You have confidence stemming from your background and feel grateful for the opportunities and connections it has given you. You realize that your heritage has been an advantage in your life, important in defining who you are, propelling your career and receiving opportunities.

You like traditions and like to maintain them in your life, whether it's family events, being active with your college alumni program, or keeping in touch with old business colleagues. You like to think about the past and the good old days. Compared to others, you are conservative in your values and point of view.

You are proud of your heritage, whether it's your country, accomplished family, education, or training. You can be a bit of a name dropper. Of course, you realize that some of your advantages were not "earned" and that you had a head start. Unfair as it is, sometimes you can judge others who don't have your credentials negatively.

Most of the time you:	**But sometimes you:**
■ Have a strong sense of identity	■ Focus too much on the past
■ Know what you want	■ Are a name dropper
■ Feel proud of your heritage	■ Try too hard to prove yourself and your worth

Generally people see you as:	**But you can:**
■ Traditional and conservative	■ Reminisce about the past
■ Proud of your heritage	■ Be too status conscious
■ Knowing important people	■ Be a bit of a snob

If this sounds like you, all the more reason to explore Strategy No. 9 Heritage positioning.

Where Are You from?

For many of us, country of origin is synonymous with top quality. There's an esteem and emotional connection that competitors lacking that heritage can't duplicate.

The fact that Veuve Clicquot is from the Champagne region of France gives it authenticity, caché, and preeminence that can create branding magic. Likewise, BMW and Mercedes are promoted as the peak of German engineering.

Under attack by vodka upstarts like Tito's Handmade Vodka, Absolut Vodka needed to do something to regain its leadership position in the US.

What was the positioning strategy they chose? In 2021, Absolut redesigned its iconic bottle to emphasize its Swedish country of origin.

The "Absolut Vodka" blue logo was enlarged and "Swedish Vodka" was added underneath in prominent, black type.[1]

For the first time, Absolut added a paper label near the bottom of the bottle that says "made with Swedish water & winter wheat" and "produced & bottled in the village of Åhus, Sweden."

Absolut didn't stop there in playing up its Swedish heritage and provenance. Lest someone not get it, Absolut emphasized its country of origin even more with "Country of Sweden" embossed in the glass bottle in all capital letters! Absolut also added the name of the founder, Lars Olsson Smith, to the medallion at the top.

The Heritage Advantage

Each industry has a hierarchy of companies in terms of heritage. People will be impressed if you started out consulting for McKinsey, BCG, Bain, or Deloitte, In consumer goods, it includes Procter & Gamble, Unilever, PepsiCo, Coca-Cola, Nestlé, and others.

If you're in tech, alignment with Stanford never fails to impress, even if you dropped out, as well as stints at iconic Silicon Valley companies.

Heritage is an enviable positioning advantage
because it's hard to match

The perception is that top companies and top schools attract the best and the brightest, so you must be top notch too. Companies often have elite training programs that can be important credentials.

In fact, I've known colleagues who offer to do a short consulting assignment, pro bono, at a prestigious company so they can add the company's name to their client list and marketing materials.

The Leverage of Heritage

Offspring with a family-name brand are often able to start out at third base while the rest of us have to start out on home plate.

Politicians and legislative aides promote having worked in a government role to set up successful consultancies. Or they can use their special heritage to angle for a senior job in the private sector heading up government relations or PR.

Many executives even get executive MBAs or take management and leadership programs so they can burnish their brand by aligning with a prestigious school.

I had no family heritage connections, but I took advantage of my educational heritage when I was unable to view paintings in private collections, for my PhD dissertation in Japanese art history.

First, I asked my professor to write a letter of introduction. Then, I had a business card printed up in English and Japanese, listing my educational credentials and scholarship: PhD student, Harvard University; Japanese Ministry of Education Fellowship; foreign exchange student Tokyo University.

Was it over the top? In America, yes. In Japan, no. In the US, we admire the bootstrapper, but Japan is a country that values heritage. And honestly, I doubt that I could have succeeded in getting access to private collections without a heritage connection.

Did it work? You bet.

Top Heritage Pathways

- Country or place of origin
- Prestigious schools
- Ethnic identity
- Impressive accomplishments
- Top-tier companies
- Awards/certifications
- Elite training
- Political/elected roles

The Heritage Story

The heritage story is about how you became who you are because of your special heritage. Your heritage story is fundamental to who you are as a person, at your core, and what you want others to believe about you. It's about why and how your heritage is so important to you.

Take time to explore how your heritage has shaped you, your values, and key decisions in your life. Find two or three stories from your childhood or adult life that demonstrate how important your background was in shaping you.

The appeal of heritage reflects our
nostalgia for "the good old days"

The heritage story often involves transformation, a defining moment that led you to your purpose and realization of the importance of your heritage. You want to give people a sense of where you came from and where you're heading.

Heritage can ignite our nostalgia for "the good old days," our longing for a simpler time that's lacking in today's more virtual, more digital, more meta world. Heritage stories are often romanticized with a sprinkling of stardust and nostalgic longing for a prior era and way of life.

Heritage Under Threat

Think of the smash-hit cable TV drama *Yellowstone,* and Kevin Costner's poignant portrayal of patriarch, John Dutton. It was initially panned by critics as "soapy trash," yet it became a word-of-mouth hit, particularly in the heartland of America.[2]

Yellowstone resonates with viewers because if its idolization of the American dream and the story of one family's struggle to retain their ranch and way of life.

The show takes place in a time when one's hertitage and identity was tied to a specific place. Most of the filming takes place outdoors against the backdrop of the snow-clad mountains of Montana.

The show captures the fear that one's heritage and way of life is under threat and whether it can survive dramatic change. It's a fear that many users of the heritage strategy have.

Becoming Michelle Obama

A coming-of-age memoir, Michelle Obama's *Becoming,* is a heritage story about her working-class upbringing and her unique African American family heritage in the South side of Chicago, and how her family molded who she became.

The focus is on her family legacy, the part of her life before her husband was elected president in 2008—the *becoming* years of her life—and all the people and events that shaped her. We meet her four-person nuclear family sharing a small, one-bedroom apartment, her great aunt Robbie who lived below them, and a cast of memorable characters.

She calls herself a "striver" and a "control freak." Obama shares the story of her high-school counselor who advised her against applying to Princeton, asserting that she would never get accepted.[3] And her determination to prove the counselor wrong. She long ago learned to recognize the "universal challenge of squaring who you are with where you come from and where you want to go."

Awards and Recognition

Awards and authentications can be an important part of the heritage strategy. There are the famous, ultra-prestigious, top awards like the Nobel Prize, Pulitzer Prize, Booker Prize, Academy Award, MacArthur Fellowship genius grant, Rhodes scholarship, and Fulbright. Winning one of them sets you apart at the peak in your industry and, no doubt, for most of us not in the realm of possibility.

In the entertainment category alone, there are dozens of awards and extravagant televised shows that we watch to see who won (and what they wore).

It's not just the blockbuster awards that count. There are hundreds of awards that celebrate talent, skills, and accomplishments on the national, regional, and local levels. Every specialty and many companies have awards and certifications. Winning one can help you advance your career, so it's worth the effort to apply. After all, if you don't go after an award, you can't get it.

If you say it, it's bragging.
If you get an award, it's an expert opinion

Awards get noticed because of their intense competition and publicity. They legitimize your achievements and abilities, since you've been recognized by an objective source. Your impressive award can give you a competitive advantage, a special heritage, and be a predictor of success.

5 Superpowers of Heritage

1. **Impressive Pedigree:** You have an impressive heritage whether it's through your family, schools, or country of origin that has given you acclaim, admiration, and an edge in your career.
2. **Impeccable Credentials and Track Record:** You don't need to toot your own horn. You have proof: a heritage and credentials that demonstrate your abilities.
3. **Highly Visible and Well Known:** Because of your heritage, you are a boldfaced name, well known in various circles as a person of importance.
4. **Cultural Traditions and Values:** You are a strong believer in passing down cultural traditions such as customs, morals, values, and beliefs, from generation to generation.
5. **Impeccable Grooming and Executive Presence:** Executive presence isn't just how you see yourself (and you're super confident), it's how others see you. And you impress with a powerful presence.

Exercise: Heritage Personal Brand Statement

Competitive Analysis

- **Identify others with a strong heritage and what they stand for:** In your industry, company, or selected arena
- **How is your special heritage different?** Write down your thoughts.

Target Audience

- **Identify who you want to reach:** Be specific, such as your boss, colleagues, customers, etc. Visualize their identity, personality, values, and lifestyle.
- **How is your heritage an advantage?** Write down your thoughts.

Example: A government relations executive wanted to position himself around his heritage of working in government at the national, regional, and local government level.

Initial Sentence: For (<u>potential business clients, media</u>) who needs (<u>business insight on government relations</u>) I stand for (<u>national, regional, and local expertise</u>)

Final Sample Positioning Sentence:

Government Relations expert with a unique heritage in local, regional, and national government.

Your Heritage Positioning Statement: Use the format below to explore Heritage positioning for Brand You by putting together a draft statement:

Draft Statement: For (<u>target audience</u>) who needs (<u>problem you solve</u>) I stand for (<u>value proposition</u>)

Final Heritage Positioning Statement _____

- **Identify three reasons to believe:** List your Heritage credentials, lineage, accomplishments, experiences, or unique background as proof of your Heritage positioning.
- **List three keywords:** Words and phrases that convey your Heritage positioning.

The Heritage Brand in a Nutshell

Heritage Brand Idea: Impressive heritage that offers an advantage

Values: Tradition, authenticity, credentials

Motivation: Strong desire to carry on traditional values and family legacy

Brand voice: Tell it like it is, passionate

Ideal customers: People who recognize the value of heritage and breeding

Battle cry: Don't underestimate the importance of heritage.

Chapter 13

Positioning Strategy No. 10 Cause

For many people, doing something significant for the greater good is as important, or even more important, than achieving the standard definition of success.

Rather than the slow slog up the corporate ladder, you have the opportunity to do something meaningful, and opportunities abound around every corner in the non-profit world.

Being synonymous with a cause has propelled many people onto a bigger stage. Think of Pakistani activist and Nobel Peace Prize laureate Malala Yousafzai (known primarily as "Malala") and the fight for girls' education, and the Swedish activist Greta Thunberg and climate change.

For young entrepreneurs, giving back or standing for a cause can be a key part of their business plan. Look at my Warby Parker glasses. It has a "Buy a Pair, Give a Pair" program. Buy one, and Warby gives the gift of sight to someone in need somewhere in the world. So far they've distributed over 10 million free pairs of glasses.

Warby Parker is a Certified B Corporation, which ensures social responsibility within the supply chain. It is lowering its carbon footprint to become one of the few carbon neutral companies.

For you too, being a crusader for a cause that's important to you may not only define your values as a leader, but propel your success.

Are You a Champion of a Cause?

Is there a special cause that you are passionate about?

Is there a new cause or niche that needs addressing?

Do you have a history of philanthropy?

Do you have a novel idea for solving a social problem?

Have you accomplished something important for a cause?

If you answered yes to two or more of these questions, then you may want to position yourself using Strategy No. 10 Cause positioning.

Cause Positioning: The cause or issue I could champion is
_____ because _____

The Cause Personality

People who adopt Cause positioning prefer doing something meaningful over just making money. You believe in devoting yourself to helping others and eliminating problems and injustice. You are committed to a cause that you believe will make a difference, even change the world.

Your definition of a life well lived is to help others achieve happiness and success, and to make the world better in some significant way. You're very empathetic and react emotionally when you see unfairness or the suffering of others. You are a benefactor to organizations and nonprofits that have similar values.

On the other hand, you can have a hard time expressing your own needs. Often, you suppress your own problems in order to help others, and that can be a problem.

Sometimes you feel overwhelmed and under too much pressure from the requests of others, but you have a hard time saying no. You worry that you won't be appreciated by others if you don't respond or aren't available to help out.

The bottom line is, your mission is to help others and make a difference in the world.

Most of the time you:	*But sometimes you:*
■ Are associated with a cause	■ Feel upset if you can't help
■ Enjoy giving more than receiving	■ Are frustrated you can't do more
■ Are admired for your cause work	■ Hide problems you have

Generally people see you as:	*But you can:*
■ Having a cause you care about	■ Sacrifice your needs for others
■ Motivated by doing good and making a difference	■ Get carried away with your cause
■ Having high ethical standards	■ Expect others to care like you do
■ Trustworthy, reliable and always willing to help out	■ Be overwhelmed with requests

If this sounds like you, all the more reason to explore positioning yourself based on Positioning Strategy No. 10 Cause positioning.

Branding a Cause

Branding tools like slogans, songs, special colors, and clothes can play a role in galvanizing people to join a social movement. Often, what can give the cause power is what people can see, hear, and feel on an emotional level.

The women's suffrage movement was a triumph for *fashion branding*. During their decades-long fight for the right to vote, suffragettes were stereotyped in the press, and it wasn't a pretty picture. So rather than take the bait, suffragettes resisted the dowdy caricatures in the press and adopted a fashionable image.

Suffragettes urged their supporters to wear three colors: purple for loyalty and dignity, white for purity, and green for hope. They were not all dressed just in solid white that is associated with women's equality today.

The leading department stores of the day made tri-color-striped ribbons for hats, belts, and badges, and handbags, shoes, and dresses in the movement's colors. It was a classy visual identity and attracted many women to the suffragettes' cause of enfranchisement for women.

From Songs to Hashtags

It's hard to think of the American Civil Rights movement without the emotional impact of Martin Luther King's "I Have a Dream" speech. Or not to visualize the marches, with people singing the cause's song, "We Shall Overcome," with crossed hands.

Today, social media is the modern way for causes and social movements to organize and mobilize. We're more likely to see *hashtag activism*, a hashtag being the linchpin to a cause taking hold and spreading around the world, as with #MeToo.

Hashtag Activism
#MeToo #BLM

The hashtag #MeToo was first used on social media as a shoutout to women who had been sexually harassed or assaulted, to call out their attackers. Women shared their stories on Twitter. Celebrities jumped into the #MeToo movement too and posted their narratives, often unlocking repressed emotions of anger, sadness, and fear.

#MeToo taught us the power of narrative and celebrity participation in creating a social movement that goes viral.

Don't Be Without a Cause

For many celebrities and leaders, a cause is a core part of their professional identity. When Stella McCartney, a committed vegan, launched her fashion company, she condemned the use of leather, fur, and PVC, an unusual branding strategy at the time. And Prince Charles has long championed climate change.

During the pandemic, the singer Dolly Parton donated $1 million to help fund coronavirus vaccine research. Now at Vanderbilt, there is a plaque citing "The Dolly Parton Covid-19 Research Fund," which led some of her fans to reword the refrain to her hit "Jolene" with the word "vaccine."

CEO activism is on the rise. PR agencies are creating entire practices around CEO activism. Marc Benoit, CEO of Salesforce, launched a homelessness initiative in San Francisco where the company is headquartered and homelessness is an acute problem.

Stand for Something

It's not easy to advocate for a cause and then rise to the very top in your profession like Ruth Bader Ginsburg did.

I love her story. While at Harvard Law, a professor criticized her for taking up a "man's spot." She transferred to Columbia Law to be near her husband and graduated first in her class, in 1959.

You would think she would be a sought-after lawyer with her credentials, but that isn't what happened. She couldn't find a job practicing law. Not one law firm in New York City would hire her, because she was a woman.[1]

So, what did she do? Ginsburg decided to teach, first at Rutgers then at Columbia Law. It was the 1960s and early 1970s, and litigation and protests on women's rights and gender equality were plentiful. While she was still teaching, Ginsburg got involved in helping the American Civil Liberties Union (ACLU) write briefs for the equal rights cases, and in 1972, she cofounded the Women's Rights Project at the ACLU.

A Cause With a Connection

Ginsburg knew all about gender inequality from her own experience trying to get hired as a lawyer. But making women's rights your cause was a risky move at the time. It was considered too progressive and way out there.

But that didn't deter Ginsburg. She had discovered her cause.

Little by little, case by case, Ginsburg changed gender discrimination in the US. She argued six equal rights cases in front of the Supreme Court and won them all.

The Branding of RBG

In 1993, Ruth Bader Ginsburg became the second woman on the Supreme Court, after Sandra Day O'Connor. One of the first concerns she weighed in on was bringing a touch of sartorial branding to the court attire of the women justices.

Let's be honest, the robes judges wear don't have much fashion or branding appeal. The standard black robe is designed for a man, with a neck opening for a man's tie and shirt collar to peek through.

But what about the ladies? Ginsburg had an idea. She introduced the white lace collar, or *jabot,* similar to the one female judges in France wore. Ginsburg amassed a dazzling array of neck pieces and realized they had branding potential way beyond making a feminine fashion statement.

Visuals Speak Louder than Words

For dissent opinions, Ginsburg wore her "dissent" collar with spikes and colored stones from Banana Republic. It looked a bit dangerous and quickly conveyed her prickly disapproval. When she wanted to channel her approval of the majority opinion, she wore the gold "majority opinion" collar that was given to her by her clerks. Through the years she amassed hundreds of collars, often gifts from admirers.

A double-barreled last name can be
hard to recall without a shortcut like RBG

A female law student gave her the nickname "the Notorious RBG," and the branding stuck. Double last names can be difficult to remember, so the initials RBG were smart from a personal-branding perspective. (Note: Alexandria Ocasio-Cortez's name is a mouthful too, and she has been given the branding shortcut AOC.)

RBG became known for her cause, women's rights, her dissents, and her neck pieces. You know you're a brand when you're impersonated on *Saturday Night Live* in a black robe with a frilly white *jabot,* oversize glasses, pulled-back hair, and saying, "I dissent."

Kim K's Got a Cause

Many know Kim Kardashian from the long-running TV reality show *Keeping Up with the Kardashians* or the saga of her life as an A-List celebrity with 65 million Twitter followers.

She's one of those celebrities who is famous for being famous. In short, she is a brand. And she's spun her reality-show fame into a number of businesses and brands, including SKIMS shapeware, KKW Fragrance, and KKW Beauty.

But now Kardashian is also woman on a mission with one of the largest megaphones on the planet. Her aim is to fix the US criminal justice system. Her focus is freeing one prisoner at a time who deserves a second chance.[2]

The first prisoner she sought to release was Alice Marie Johnson, a 64-year-old great-grandmother from Tennessee, who was sentenced to life in prison without parole on drug charges. After being incarcerated for 21 years, Kardashian felt that Johnson had paid her debt to society.

Your Cause Action Plan

Kardashian has become a force in prison reform. She has successfully lobbied former president Trump, phoned governors and legislators, written clemency petitions, and paid the legal fees for prisoners she's trying to get pardoned.

She's relentlessly championing her cause on social media. She produced a documentary, *The Justice Project.* Kardashian even had Johnson model her SKIMS shapewear in a TV commercial.

And Kardashian is getting results. She has already helped release dozens of people who were incarcerated.

"Why This Is My Cause" Story

Celebrity activism has a long history in America, from Jane Fonda to George Clooney to Angelina Jolie. Awareness is critical for any cause, so celebrity activism can be a game changer.

A good cause rounds out one's brand. It adds a caring, giving-back patina to one's personal brand that's outside of one's career achievements.

So sometimes you can feel skeptical, "Is the cause really meaningful to them, or is it calculated celebrity window dressing?"

Kardashian admits that her own team of advisers had been telling her to adopt a cause for some time. One of their suggestions was Operation Smile, which performs surgery on children with cleft palates. Many of the causes presented to her seemed worthy, but none really clicked, until Kardashian saw, where else but on Twitter, a video about Alice Marie Johnson.

> Your cause can be anything you're
> passionate about that needs a champion

But why prison reform? It hardly seems like a natural fit. Kardashian says part of the attraction is her four African American children, and most of the prisoners she's trying to free are African American. She was interested in the law as a teenager, but her father discouraged her.

So in a way, Kardashian is coming full circle to an earlier career vision. She's excited about everything she's learning about the law. She's even studying law, not full-time but through a State Bar of California program. She passed one of her two bar exams (after three failed attempts).

Lead a Cause at Work

A technology employee, Michael, set up a Black Employee Resource Group (ERG) at his company, promoting leadership development, mentoring, and events for African American employees, an underrepresented group at his company.

Black ERGs were the first affiliate group organized around a shared identity, and today progressive companies have ERGs for many different types of groups by race, gender, and other affiliations.

Having more diversity representation in leadership roles is Michael's passion and an important issue in many companies. Playing such a visible role in the Black ERG has been great for his visibility as well. He's developed relationships with people with similar values throughout the organization, brought in outside minority speakers at events, and set up networking and other programs.

5 Super Powers of Cause Positioning

1. **A Leader with Purpose, Mission, and Values:** As a leader you stand out because of your sense of purpose, mission, and values, which you believe are important to the success of every organization. You want to make the world a better place.

2. **Deep Passion for Your Cause:** You are aligned with a cause that has special meaning for you personally and defines you on a larger stage. You are very knowledgeable about your cause and have a strong record of accomplishment.

3. **Articulate Spokesperson with a Strong PR Platform:** Your PR platform is not about you but something loftier, a cause that's important. You're able to get your points across to the media clearly and memorably, and get positive coverage. You're not afraid to answer hard questions.

4. **Strong Empathy and Connection to Others:** You are an empathetic leader with a genuine interest in your team, its challenges and feelings. You realize that at the end of the day, it's the emotional needs of the team that are important, not just productivity.

5. **Driven to Change the World:** You feel confident and hopeful that you can change the world. Motivated more by ideals than financial gain. You realize that true change takes time and you have the determination, charisma, and grassroots organizing skills to attract others to your cause. You have a wider network than most people, because

of your activism. You're gregarious and good at social gatherings and networking.

Exercise: Cause Personal Brand Statement

Competitive Analysis

- **Identify two or three people you admire**. People with a strong affiliation with a cause: Analyze what they stand for and how they are effective in leading their cause.
- **How are you and your cause different?** Write down your thoughts.

Target Audience

- **Identify who you want to reach.** Be specific, such as the nonprofit community, your boss, colleagues, customers, etc. Visualize their identity, personality, values, and lifestyle.
- **How will your cause appeal to them?** Write down your thoughts.

Sample Positioning Sentence

Example: A financial advisor who wanted to give back to the community came up with financial literacy for high school students.

Initial sentence: For (<u>high school students</u>) who need (<u>to understand how to make, save, and invest money</u>) I stand for (<u>a financial adviser who can show teenagers how to earn, save, and invest money</u>)

Final Sample Positioning Sentence: Financial adviser changing the way teens save, invest, and think about money

Your Cause Positioning Statement: Select your cause and use the format below to explore Cause positioning for Brand You by putting together a draft statement.

Draft Statement: For (<u>target audience</u>) who needs (<u>problem you solve</u>) I stand for (<u>value proposition</u>)

Final Cause Positioning Statement _____

- **Identify Three Reasons to Believe:** List your cause and related experience or other credentials, accomplishments, experiences, or different point of view or approach to the cause.
- **List Three Keywords:** Showcase three adjectives or phrases as keywords for this positioning and your cause.

The Cause Brand in a Nutshell

Cause Brand Idea: You and your cause will make a difference in the world.

Values: Helping others, making the world a better place

Motivation: Passion for your cause, quest to make a difference in the world

Brand voice: Caring, passionate

Ideal customers: People who share your passion for your cause

Battle cry: Together we can make a difference.

PART III:
GIVING BRAND YOU THE WOW FACTOR

Chapter 14

Visual Identity: Your Silent Communicator That Speaks Loudly Through Your Presence, Style, Clothes, Hair, Imagery, and Color Palette

You've done the hard work, the strategic part of branding. You've analyzed Brand You and studied the Top Ten Brand Positioning Strategies. You've selected the best positioning concept for Brand You.

Now comes the creative part of branding.

Crafting Your *Look and Feel*

Following the branding model, you need to package Brand You with a unique *look and feel*. A brand's packaging and design speak to us quickly and emphatically through imagery, color, shape, material, and typography.

> Your brand's look and feel reflects what people
> see *and* feel when they interact with Brand You

It's the same with people. Done successfully, your brand's look and feel ties everything together—your positioning, how you look to others (in person and virtually), and how people feel when they connect with Brand You.

You just have a couple of seconds to create impact when you meet someone new or enter an Instagram profile. That impact is powered by your look and feel. It's that important.

Visuals Are Silent Ambassadors

We are visual people and we connect with the world through visual clues. Your personal brand's look and feel reflects not just what people *see* when they meet you, but how they *feel* emotionally when they interact with you. So it's a powerful tool for connecting with others and conveying the message you want to communicate about Brand You.

Realize, too, that making focused decisions about how you come across isn't about being fake. It's about being authentic but also savvy. When a brand really clicks, the visual and the verbal message are one. That's your goal too.

How Do People See You?

You win or lose based on how others see you. The perceptions of others are the perceptions that count in the branding world.

If you want people to think you are creative,
you have to look creative

Everything communicates visually—from your shoes to your hair style, from your background setting for Zoom calls to your website.

Visual identity tells us whether you are powerful or wacky, the girl next door or a glamourous diva, creative or conservative.

Branding Power of Wearables

It may seem superficial, but your clothes are one of the loudest talkers in the personal branding tool kit. For centuries, clothing was a wearable status symbol and there was a strict social hierarchy that dictated who could wear what. Clothes told where you stood on the status totem pole. That's why luxury clothing was regulated.

In Tudor England, only nobles could wear silk, velvet, and fur. These luxury items were off-limits for the butcher's wife even if her husband could afford it. It was illegal because you would be presenting yourself as something you're not. The messaging value of clothes was not lost on Renaissance Florence ruler Cosimo de' Medici, who remarked, "One can make a gentleman from two yards of red cloth."[1]

In modern times, "power clothes" can give you a status boost, too, particularly in the office. Power clothing can make you feel more confident, and project strength and authority. It's also been linked to increased productivity and better negotiating skills. The key is choosing clothes that best fit your personality and the message you want to convey.

The New Power Office Casual

After dressing from the waist up and switching tailored suits and dresses for athleisure, what's next, sartorially? What will be the long-term effect of the pandemic in the way we dress for work?

There's been a casualization taking place in work attire that was initiated in Silicon Valley in the early 1980s. Then the trend spiraled across the land during the pandemic when tens of millions of workers set up shop at home.

Power dressing for today's office is still being defined, but one thing is clear: there is little interest in stiff fabrics, formal styles, and tight clothes like before. Employees report that they will be dressing more casually and comfortably when they return to the office.[2] Many white collar workers say that they are done with belts, ties, and dress shoes.

The new power clothes are a mash-up of Zoom and the office—a high-status comfort wear—that convey, "I'll do the work but I'm going to be comfortable doing it" vibe. Power casual clothes are comfortable, with elastic waist bands, relaxed tailoring, and soft fabrics, yet polished enough to make you feel put together at work.

It's a hybrid clothing solution for the hybrid office. No one is likely to feel out of place, clothing-wise working from home or the office. From a branding perspective, though, you want to give business casual your own vibe.

Dressing to Stand Out

Capitol Hill is a place known for its traditions, rules, and protocols. Male members dress in tailored suits. The women usually dress for obscurity, or at least with a tasteful sartorial subtlety. (Think of the dark pantsuits favored by Vice President Kamala Harris.)

It was not a place for standing out with eyebrow-raising clothes, until Kyrsten Sinema, the first woman to represent Arizona in the Senate, came along.

At her Senate swearing in, she was reminiscent of Marilyn Monroe with her platinum curls and stilettos.[3] She swept into the Senate chamber in a white-caped outfit (wink to the suffragettes) for Donald Trump's first impeachment trial.

Hit the Spotlight: Center Stage

Sinema presided over Congress in a hot pink sweater with the words "Dangerous Creature" on the front. Then, there was the denim vest she wore when presiding over the Senate. Yes, denim. It set the media ablaze. (By the way, denim is against the Senate dress code.)

Her clothes are so quirky and flamboyant with their mix-match prints and candy-colored party wigs that I've often wondered, "How does she concoct these outfits?" Then I think, "Keep the clothes coming, Kyrsten. You're on center stage and everyone is watching."

Sinema is a maverick. She likes to stand out in a crowd. She's a free thinker and not a fan of convention, either in clothes and hairstyles or following along party lines on Democratic initiatives. She wants to be in control, her own person.

Hair Branding

Hair, for women, has often been an expression of beauty. Your hair says a lot about you, too, just like clothes. Since women's hairstyle possibilities are endless, it's easier to say a lot or to trip up.

The key for women and men is to have a current hairstyle, lest you come across as out of touch. And avoid extreme styles and bird of paradise colors unless you want to brand yourself as a maverick or work in a creative field.

Studies on appropriate hairstyles for women in the office recommend short cuts ("professional") over long hair ("young"), and straight hair ("serious") over curly dos ("unruly").[4]

But there's a transformation taking place on what's acceptable. Look at the diversity of women's hairstyles in the media, government, and business, even at the highest levels.

Historically, there was discrimination against Black natural hairstyles, and many Black women straightened their hair for what was perceived to be a "more professional" look. Thankfully, these racist stereotypes are being squashed. A number of states have passed the CROWN Act (Creating a Respectful and Open World for Natural Hair), the first legislation to ban discrimination on hair style.[5]

Channeling Who?

The men are giving the women a run for their money on the hair front these days. The media stories on UK Prime Minister Boris Johnson often mention his unruly mane. It's easy to see why. Watching the prime minister in the media, it's easy to wonder, "What's with the hair?"

You can interpret Johnson's hair as smart personal branding, positioning him as a maverick. The unconventional vibe is particularly compelling when Johnson polishes off the look with a rumpled suit.

Then there's Silicon Valley's Jack Dorsey, former CEO of Twitter and current CEO of Block (formerly named Square). When he testified virtually before the Senate Commerce Committee in 2020, social media went wild over his long, mangy "pandemic" beard. Even his mother weighed in to say that she hated it.

From a visual identity standpoint, Dorsey presents his brand as a mash-up of a rugged mountain man and a Zen monk, as someone who's left the cares and phoniness of the mortal world behind.

Dorsey has an unconventional lifestyle, for a man who used to be CEO to two Silicon Valley tech companies. Now he's running just one. He's down to a lone, one meal a day. He does an "extremely painful" form of meditation and kicks off each day with an ice bath. Even in Silicon Valley, he stands out a maverick.[6]

A Dose of Dazzle

Look at your wardrobe and your style. What do you want your visual identity to say about you? Is it consistent with your personal brand strategy?

Is there a signature feature or trademark accessory you can use to heighten your visual identity? Think Madeleine Albright's brooches or Meghan Markle's stilettos. Or colorful, oversize glasses, like with Iris Apfel or Seth Godin. Or a trademark hairstyle? (Think Jennifer Aniston or Queen Elizabeth.)

What visual attributes do people compliment you on? How can you emphasize your good points?

These are all questions you will want to explore if you want to maximize your visual identity. If you don't communicate the right message, send out confusing messages, or fade into the wallpaper, you are undercutting your effectiveness with a milquetoast visual identity.

Branding in the Metaverse

The metaverse is the new frontier in personal branding. You can craft your personal brand any way you want in the metaverse. You could build your avatar's visual identity based on the way you look in real life (a little thinner perhaps). Or you can stand out with a fantasy image or any image you've concocted to symbolize Brand You.

Above all, you want your virtual and physical brand to come from your positioning strategy. You'll confuse everyone with scattered, opposing brand messages. Your avatar and virtual environment should convey a unified brand idea.

What to Wear in the Metaverse

Mark Zuckerberg wore his trademark uniform of black jeans, white sneakers, and a navy T-shirt for his virtual announcement of Facebook's name change to Meta in October 2021. He had other choices, though. In his virtual closet, you could see an astronaut suit and skeleton costume.

The metaverse is just in its initial stages but already there is a fashion infrastructure being built around it with over 100 fashion brands so far.[7] Nike has launched a virtual sneaker brand.

There are even the virtual version of *haute couture*—brands backed by the blockchain and owned by a single person. Mass market fashion is off chain and available to one and all. Some ready-to-wear fashion companies are hiring designers trained in virtual design so they can offer clothes for the virtual world and the real world.

It's an exciting or scary new world depending on your age and outlook. In developing your avatar, you want the virtual and the physical, and the visual and the verbal to be seamlessly intertwined with a distinctive message.

Everything On Brand?

Your brand positioning strategy is your foundation for your visual identity. You want every visual element to be *on brand* so everything is consistent and works together to convey your brand message.

If someone deviates from their established persona,
we're confused, and we even question our trust in them

If you are not consistent across all channels of communication, people won't know what to make of you. You bewilder people if you have one visual identity in person and a different one online, or a different one on LinkedIn from your profile on Twitter.

You might as well be speaking gibberish, since you will only be causing havoc with your brand identity. People want honesty and authenticity—the real deal—with everything consistent with one unified message.

Your Visual Aesthetic

Imagine how different the design for your website, video background, presentation decks, even your clothes, would be if your defining positioning is the Leader or the Maverick or the Expert or the Elite (or any of the other positioning strategies).

One useful tool from the design playbook is to develop a *mood board,* or *inspiration board.* It's a collection of images, colors, lifestyle photos, fonts, and website design to help you visualize your personal brand look. It's worth taking the time to put together since just the act of doing a mood board will focus you and lead to new visual ideas. (You can do it on a physical board or online on Pinterest.)

A Mood Board: a collection of images, colors, photos, and font(s) that capture your visual aesthetic

---

Include a collage of the keywords you selected for your brand positioning for inspiration and to keep you on track with your positioning.

The Enduring First Impression

You have just a couple of seconds to generate a positive impression when people first meet you in person or interact virtually. The impact of that first impression is generated largely through visual information people take in about you: how you look, what you're wearing, your facial expression and hairstyle, and the lighting and background if it's a video call.

What's fascinating is that these blink-of-an-eye first impressions are very sticky. They are not likely to change much over time, unless you do something dramatic to change them.

So the first impression you make is either launching a great relationship or closing the door on one. It's that important.

If you're meeting with a new customer, a senior leader, or a recruiter online, you may worry because your first encounter is virtual. Transitioning between virtual and in-person is part of our business lives now, so leave enough prep time to make sure your lighting and tech are running smoothly.

The Attractiveness Advantage

Like great art, great design or packaging gets us to slow down and admire it. How many people, like me, have chosen to buy a wine because we loved the label design? Or buy a product because we like the packaging? Or feel more confident because we look good on a particular day?

It's human nature to be attracted to good-looking things. Even babies are more attracted to appealing faces. Locking onto the attractive people in a group stays with us as we grow older. Lovely things have a way of grabbing our attention.

Attractiveness also has the advantage of the *halo effect*. Like it or not, looking good gives you a career boost just like attractively packaged brands get a boost. Attractive people tend to be viewed as smarter, more likable, more successful, better in so many ways—all attributes that have nothing to do with looks, obviously.

Hacking the Beauty Principle

So what do you do if looks are not your strong suit? Give up?

One group of researchers determined that projecting confidence is attractive.[8] They found that coaching people to present themselves assertively and confidently overturns the attractiveness bias.

Projecting confidence reads as attractive

Besides, in my view, everyone can be attractive. It's all about making the most of what you have. Looking interesting and having a distinct personal style is attractive. Feeling that you look your best boosts your performance, studies show. Having a welcoming and empathetic personality makes you likable, and that is very attractive.

Look at successful people in business, nonprofits, entertainment, or whatever. It's clear that we have a much more inclusive definition of what's attractive and who rises to the top. Having a unique visual identity sets you apart, and that's always good in personal branding.

Radical Makeover

Rarely has there been as educational an example of the power of visual identity as the radical before-and-after makeover of Elizabeth Holmes during her fraud trial in 2021.

We first got to know the beautiful, genius CEO of Theranos in the media, including the magazine covers of *Fortune, Forbes,* and *Inc.*

From a visual identity standpoint, she stood out not just because she was super attractive, but for her appropriation of Steve Jobs's black turtleneck uniform, boldly accented with bright red lipstick and sleek blond hair. (In one interview before the trial, Holmes showed a closet with over 150 black turtlenecks.)

In her trial, we saw a complete do-over of Holmes's image.[9] Gone was the Technicolor. Now, we had the chamomile tea version of Elizabeth Holmes. Her visual identity was sartorially bland with nondescript, business casual shirts and skirts. Her hair was in soft curls. Gone were the black turtlenecks, red lipstick, straightened hair, and spike heels.

Formerly positioned as Wonder Woman, Holmes was now the Girl Next Door.

Each day of the trial we saw her enter and leave the courtroom holding hands with her mother and partner. Oh, and she often carried a new trademark accessory, a diaper bag backpack, a reference to the baby she'd had in the summer.

It seemed like a case of the defense using the principles of visual identity to mount a campaign of relatability for the jury. But visual identity can only get you so far. It has to match your actions or there is a brand disconnect, as Elizabeth Holmes discovered when she was found guilty of fraud.

We're All on Camera Now

Zoom is the great equalizer. You're not meeting with your boss across a desk that implies superior status. Everyone's box is the same size. You're included in meetings that you wouldn't be in if it involved travel.

When you pick out your clothes for a video call, you also need to think about what colors and styles would look good on a screen.

Look at TV anchors, reporters, and pundits who come under a lot of scrutiny. The women choose bright, solid colors that pop. They avoid patterns that distract and neutrals and pastels, which dull one's appearance. Check out how you look on your laptop webcam or your phone camera. You can look great in person but completely different on a screen, especially if you don't have good lighting.

Curate Your Background

Your background is saying something about you too. Think of your video call background as a stage set. Is it conveying the impression you want?

It can be smart to include elements in your professional space that communicate who you are. But keep it simple, as too many decorative pieces can be distracting.

If you're positioning yourself as an expert, you can set up your video call in front of your bookcase. If you are an innovative, creative type, you'll want to have a more creative background such as floating shelves and objet d'art. Good lighting is key. Most important, make sure your light source is in front of you. North-facing natural light is best. Lacking that, use LED bulbs with warm light.

The Branded Presentation

An online presentation can start to seem remote and impersonal like a prerecorded video, unless you make it more personal. You need to draw attention to yourself, your face, and expressions, and connect by looking directly into the camera.

The best online presentations are simple and visual. Don't cram too many bullet points or text into your slides. Use a large font and bold visuals.

Visuals make information easy to remember and keep your presentation entertaining. You can visualize data with graphs or use photos to illustrate an idea or tell a story. Your audience needs to look at a slide and get the message quickly. Otherwise, it's spam.

It can be hard to keep your audience engaged when you can't engage them face-to-face, so you need to make your slides interactive by asking questions and having people respond on Chat.

The Communication Power of Visual Identity

Before the conflict in Ukraine exploded in 2022, the Ukrainian president Volodymyr Zelenskyy wore suits and ties to address the nation from his ornate presidential office like any country's leader. Since the invasion, Zelenskyy retired his suits and replaced them with the work-a-day garb of a military man—an olive green tee, often with a cross over the heart, the insignia of the Ukrainian military.

It's become an iconic image of the conflict: Day after day the solitary image of President Zelenskyy wearing a simple olive green shirt in a stark, bunker-like room with the Ukrainian flag beside him addressing his people or speaking to the British Parliament, the European Parliament, and the American Congress.

With his background as an actor, he no doubt understands the power of presence and that what you wear and your environment speaks volumes. His army green shirt connects him to the military and telegraphs the conflict he faces. It communicates that he is a hands-on man of the people, not an elite far away and protected from the conflict. It communicates that he shares the strength, resolve and patriotism of his countrymen. His visual image locks in the "narrative of a Russian Goliath and Ukrainian David, of hubris vs. heroism."[10]

10 Tips for Your Visual Identity

Here are ten tips to keep in mind as you develop your visual identity in person and virtually:

1. *Have a consistent visual identity in person and online:* Don't send mixed messages.

2. *Align your visual identity with your brand positioning:* Your visual identity should come from your positioning strategy. Revisit the choice you made in the Top Ten Positioning Strategies.

3. *Put together a mood board or inspiration board:* Creating a mood board is worth the extra time, because it will help you focus on a coordinated visual identity for Brand You.

4. *Think of your background on video calls as a stage set or store front:* Everyone is going to scrutinize your background, so keep it simple and plain so the focus is on your face. Or use the backdrop to tell a story through artwork, books, or objects.

5. *Crack the new code of business casual and make it yours:* We're in an era when most of us can dress in business casual every day. Don't neglect the branding power of clothes and hairstyles. Find a way to make your style come through.

6. *Redefine beauty:* Projecting confidence and looking interesting is the new black. Project your own authentic style.

7. *Select a signature item:* Brands like to stand out with a signature logo or design feature, and you should too. It could be your glasses, a scarf, shoes, clothes—whatever feels right for you.

8. *Have a trademark color or color palette:* An effective way to unify your brand is through a coordinated palette.

9. *Craft an avatar for the virtual world:* Create an avatar that connects with your positioning and feels like you.

10. *Choose a strong visual approach for presentations and slide decks:* Make yourself the star. Go light on text and heavy on pictures on your slides.

The whole purpose of visual identity is to maximize the non-verbal message you are sending about yourself. Does your brand message on the outside match your personal brand on the inside?

Chapter 15

Customizing Your Verbal Identity Through Names, Story, Taglines, Point of View, and Voice

The counterpart to visual identity in brand building is verbal identity. The articulation of names, stories, special words, points of view, taglines, content, and voice bring a brand to life. In today's global and digitally connected workplace, your words and voice can be more powerful than ever.

If you experienced the Oscar-winning performance of Colin Firth as the stuttering King George in *The King's Speech*, you experienced the frustration of not being able to communicate with your target audience. It's that painful feeling when your lack of confidence or ability destroys the message you want to communicate.

Record Your Voice

Close your eyes and listen to how you sound. Warning, it may not be a positive experience the first time. I thought it was a completely different person, the first time I heard my recorded voice.

Your voice is unique, so you need to understand its one-of-a-kind sound. Evaluate your voice's speed, pitch, energy, and attractiveness. Is it nasal or deep? What do you like about your voice? What are its flaws? Are you often asked to repeat what you said? If so, what do you plan to do about it?

Even an A-list talent like Justin Timberlake took voice lessons to deepen his voice. So you're in good company if you decide to work with a voice coach to maximize your voice's impact.

Your Voice Deserves to be Heard

People with deep voices command attention, sound confident, and have credibility—all valuable characteristics for professional people. So you won't be surprised to hear that CEOs with deep, what I call business-school voices, ran larger companies, were paid more, and had longer careers.[1]

Successful men and women both stand out
in one important voice trait—vocal energy

Although most women can't match men on the Hz scale measuring pitch, successful men and women both stand out in one important voice trait—*vocal energy*. When you have high vocal energy, you easily take your voice from high to low, from forceful to soft, from fast to slow, depending on the emotions you want to express and what you want to emphasize. It's an advantage, because an energetic voice reads as authentic and inspires trust, according to experts.[2]

First Time I Heard Your Voice

So what really matters, more than your actual voice being deep, is *how* you say what you say. It's your rhythm, inflections, and cadence (the mixing up of vocal expression) that sway us to listen carefully to what is being said.

The power of the human voice is not surprising when you consider that for centuries, there was no written language. People listened to one another's voices. Even some dating websites, like Hinge, have added voice recordings so choosing a date is not just about the picture and written profile. And your voice can help attract a partner. Hinge users are 1.4 times more likely to go on a date if they've matched up through the voice recording prompts.[3]

Fortunately, vocal energy is something that we can all practice and add to our repertoire.

And, at the very least, don't speak in a monotone or read off a script rather than speaking directly with your eyes on the audience. Both are low vocal energy choices.

Voice as Brand

Your voice is a powerful tool—a superpower—for personal branding.

Your voice is special. No other voice is exactly like yours. The challenge is to use your voice to convey your unique brand personality through how you *sound* and the *words* you communicate.

Having a different-sounding voice can make you stand out. Think of Russia expert Fiona Hill's fact-filled testimony (she's a Harvard Ph.D.) during then President Donald Trump's first impeachment in 2019.

It was not just her stunning testimony that brought her out of obscurity and made her a star on the national stage, it was the way she communicated with her distinctive British accent (from North East Britain). Her British accent made her statements as riveting as what she said.

Power of the Podcaster

Look at the power of podcasts. No other medium is as personal or as intimate as listening to your favorite podcast. Certainly not video or printed text.

Podcasts allow you to use the power of your voice, along with your content, to communicate, and build trust and community. There is something immensely comforting to your listeners when you tell them a story, or entertain them, or educate them, or riff on daily ups-and-downs and all they have to do is listen to your voice.

By Any Other Name

Giving a brand a name is the first and most important branding decision. A great name can win customers over before they've even experienced a brand.

We all know Juliet's famous lines from *Romeo and Juliet*: "A rose by any other name would smell as sweet." But would it? I think not. I suspect a wordsmith like Shakespeare surely knew the power of a name to affect how we experience people and objects.

In fact, one team of researchers tried to settle the issue with a study of 15 different odors. The results were clear. "Attractive" odors did not smell as sweet when they were given an "ugly" name (for example, a rose with the name "rotting flower").[4] The study proved that what something is called does influence how we perceive it.

That's why marketers spend a lot of time exploring names for new products. A product's success depends upon it. A great name is a valuable asset and can practically make a brand. In some cases, there isn't much difference between two products except for their names.

The Sweetest Name

Names are important for people too. It may be unfair. After all, we don't choose our own name. Your parents give you a name when you're born. And your name can influence how people peg you and treat you, even how you feel about yourself throughout your life.

Stereotypes abound. A name can say whether you're perceived as rich or poor, native or foreign, likable or distasteful. Names can be commonplace or unusual, popular or old-fashioned. It pays to have a name that is trendy— you're more likely to be with the in crowd, too. So it's not surprising that many expectant parents scrutinize lists of popular baby names.

One test of names was done on online dating sites.[5] People with popular names like Alexander and Jennifer were chosen over competitors with more ethnic or old-fashioned-sounding names like Boris and Olga. Another test showed that even teachers were biased toward students with popular or attractive names and gave them higher scores on essays.[6]

Of course, there are many exceptions to names and their power over your destiny. Especially today, with so many people seeking unusual names for their children so that it will be easier to own your name online.

Maximize Name Power

For most of us, our birth name is our forever name, unless we change it when we get married. But if you're building a personal brand, you've got to take a hard look at your name.

Write down your name on a piece of paper. What adjectives and images come to mind? Do you like your name? What's wrong with it? Do people ask you to repeat or spell your name a lot?

Do you have a "good" name, from a branding perspective?

Good names are:
- **Short**—Think Uber or Oprah
- **Easy to say and spell**—Think Nike or Brad Pitt
- **Evocative**—Think Meta or Dolly Parton
- **Different**—Think Google or Barack Obama
- **Attractive**—Think Twitter or Meghan Markle
- **Ownable on the internet**—Your name dot com is best

Name Problems?

So what do you do if your name breaks all the good name rules? You have a "bad" name that is too long or hard to say and spell, or one that is so common there are tens of thousands of people on LinkedIn with your name.

You don't have to do anything, of course. Arnold Schwarzenegger didn't change his name, and it didn't hurt his career in movies or politics. Or you can be active on social media so that you're more likely to come up on the internet in spite of having a common or difficult name.

There are many ways to maintain the integrity of your given name, but tweak it so it works better from a branding perspective, especially if you're able to get yourname.com on the internet.

For a common name, you can include a middle name or initial to distinguish yourself in a crowded name category, like Samuel L. Jackson or Sarah Jessica Parker. Or you can stand out with an unusual spelling like Suze Orman or Barbra Streisand.

If your name is long or difficult to say or spell, you could simplify it like Gennady Vaynerchuck, who drastically simplified his first name to Gary and often goes by the shortcut Gary Vee.

You can go by your middle name to make it more memorable. Rachel Meghan Markle became Meghan Markle, and Christopher Ashton Kutcher became Ashton Kutcher. Laura Jeanne Witherspoon became Reese Witherspoon, giving herself an image boost with a more "Hollywood" feel by using her mother's maiden name as her first name.

Name Your Stuff

In today's new world of work with disperse global teams, naming a project, initiative, team, or idea is a powerful tool that helps everybody understand a project and rally around it.

Naming a project, an idea, or a point of view anchors it in people's minds and gives everyone a handle for discussing it.

It's not easy to talk in the abstract about a project like that "new product idea we're developing." A name makes a project real with an identity that people can coalesce around, like the code name "Purple" that Apple used for the first iPhone. Even the building where it was developed was called the "Purple Dorm."

A good name can even help
a project's success

A name can send signals about what a project is meant to accomplish and says it's important (at least important enough to get a name). Or the name can suggest an attribute or reference point. Animals can be good sources of project names (Jaguar, Leopard, etc.) and myths (Apollo, Mercury, etc.). Without a name, a new initiative remains half baked.

If you're leading the project, the name links you with the project's goals and becomes part of your intellectual property.

Point of View?

You can build your brand through thought leadership on your field or industry, or larger social issues of the day. Ben & Jerry's has always had a strong point of view as part of its brand narrative, which is a big part of its success.

The ice cream maker takes an omni-cause approach. The company embraced Black Lives Matter and criminal justice reform. It started a campaign on climate change through its release of a new flavor: Save Our Swirled.

It's a maverick brand that's not afraid to take a stand. The company generated quite a bit of controversy when it stopped selling ice cream in Israeli-occupied territories in 2021.

Some of our largest companies are having a social awakening, too. Driven by consumer activists, companies like Nike and Apple have come out with a point of view on sweatshop labor and poor working conditions for their products and have initiated supply-chain responsibility reports.

Other large companies, like Coca-Cola and Bank of America, are speaking out against new voting laws that will make it harder for Black voters to participate in elections. Having a point of view on the right side of justice can also lead to more profit for companies, according to a study of the Civil Rights movement in the twentieth century. When you start doing things for a cause, you get the attention of people with the same concerns.

What's Your Line?

There's not a lot of demand for sales messages. That's why marketers disguise product messages in a tagline or catch phrase or in an ad or commercial. Dressing up your message in that way is more engaging and appealing than a sales pitch could ever be. When they come up with a message that resonates, brands repeat and retell their messages so people will remember them.

Great taglines embody the unique selling proposition of the brand, like Apple's "Think Different" or Nike's "Just Do It." Aspirational taglines like these appeal to who we are on a deeper level.

Politicians are good at branding and often use catchphrases to communicate a legislative platform, like President Biden's "Build Back Better" or former president Trump's "Make America Great Again."

A supply chain manager used attribute positioning to build his reputation around the keyword "accountability." His battle cry for his team is "Everyone's accountable, everywhere, all the time." It's a phrase he uses a lot so that everyone understands the mission.

Tell a Story

Story is a lesson from the Madison Avenue advertising playbook. Marketers are master storytellers who wrap their brands in myths and stories in their advertising and promotions.

You need to be a storyteller too. If you start using a relevant and interesting story in your next presentation, chances are the one thing that people will remember is the story.

Story gives language emotional power, and emotion is the short route to the brain. Story creates movies in the mind that we can see, feel, and remember.

Story involves the left brain and the right brain. Most presentations with their facts and support points just connect with the left brain, our rational side. Story pierces the right hemisphere and makes us visualize and feel what we hear.

Story is a pull strategy. It attracts and pulls you in. Story is interactive. It gets the listener involved in connecting the dots, figuring out the meaning behind the story.

Deliver Your Story

Story writing isn't like the essay writing you did in school. You want to keep your business stories brief, about a minute or two in length, and make them emotional and exciting.

After setting the stage with a time and place, launch everything in motion with a bang. Alfred Hitchcock called this element the *MacGuffin*—the problem, decision, situation, or person that changes life for the hero (your customer, team, you, or someone you know).

You need to emphasize the unexpected obstacles that must be overcome before reaching the goal. When the problems reach their high point, the hero faces a test. It's the turning point in the story.

Alas, against all odds, the hero solves the problem.

The Origin Story

A key personal branding story to develop is your origin or purpose story. Your origin story is fundamental to who you are as a person and what is important for other people to know about you.

It's about how and why you want to create meaning in the world. It's not about making a lot of money. It's about an ideal—wanting to make the world better in some way.

Suze Orman is a personal finance guru with an in-your-face style on her cable television show and string of bestselling personal finance books.

Orman's origin story involves her family's precarious financial condition during her childhood in Chicago.

The MacGuffin, the defining moment, came when a fire engulfed her father's chicken takeout store, and he rushed back in to recover the cash register, leaving him with third-degree burns. That event set everything in motion. Orman says she learned that "money was more important than life." It was a message that she had to unlearn.

Orman struggled with making money until she changed course and started to learn about saving and investing money. Educating people about money became her passion. Orman describes her purpose in her tagline, "to change the way Americans think, talk and act about money."

Emotional Branding

Story is so powerful because logic and analysis doesn't persuade as well as emotions do. Many of the most effective advertising messages are examples of *emotional branding*. They reach out to the emotions rather than to your analytical brain. Maybe they don't even talk about or show the brand at all in the commercial. You have to wait until the end to discover the sponsoring brand.

Getting people interested in you, your ideas, or your company is emotional branding too. You get people interested in your ideas not just because of the facts but because they *feel* something about who you are, your story, and what you're talking to them about. You fascinate them with your story.

Look at the Liberty Mutual insurance commercials and the silly saga between the LiMu emu and its friend, Doug. Inspired by the buddy-cop scenario from television shows, we're captivated by an interesting story (and anthropomorphic avian character) wrapped around a dull product.

Storytelling's Dark Side

Emotional branding and storytelling techniques can have a dark side, too, if people get so wrapped up in a story that they suspend disbelief and rational analysis. And it happens.

A high-profile example of masterful verbal identity, emotional branding, and storytelling revolves around Theranos founder Elizabeth Holmes, who was convicted of four counts of fraud in 2022. (See the previous chapter, which touches on her mastery of visual identity as well.)

Holmes had a moving origin story: She was scared of needles as a child. Then she had an uncle who died at a young age of cancer. That traumatic experience led to her desire to change the way diseases are diagnosed.

Following the model of Steve Jobs and other Silicon Valley icons, Holmes dropped out of Stanford at age 19. The only missing story element was starting her business in a garage.

Master of Verbal Identity

Holmes had talented naming and tagline prowess. She named her company Theranos, an amalgam of "therapy" and "diagnosis." She named its testing device Edison, after Thomas Edison. Holmes even had a battle cry: "A single drop of blood can change the world."

She was gifted in the art of the pitch and attracted almost $1 billion from investors. She even had a low, baritone voice that some felt was fabricated to give her gravitas with investors.

Her origin story and business pitch were so emotionally compelling that many people, including sophisticated investors and top echelon government leaders, believed it: that a person with no medical background could, with a pinprick of blood, accurately test for hundreds of diseases. Unfortunately, there was little to Theranos beyond a well-told, but fictitious, story.

The Lost Art of Communication

If you want to take your brand somewhere in the world, communicating and speaking well are skills you need to master, especially after having endured the pandemic.

One survey in the fall of 2020 of nearly 33,000 college students done by three universities found that two-thirds struggled with loneliness. Many students reported feeling awkward talking in-person after the isolation of the pandemic.[7] They preferred text or social media over face-to-face interaction.

Communication skills, both online and in-person, are skills we need to get back if we want a healthy society in the future.

You'll know it when your way of communicating clicks. There will be that wonderful moment in a meeting when you feel at one with the audience. You'll know it when you're connecting—both the content and the way you deliver it is breaking through. You can feel the energy in the room.

That's when you'll know what it's like to be a powerful communicator. That's when you'll know it was worth the effort to develop your verbal edge.

Chapter 16

Marketing Brand You so That You're Visible and Relevant and You Achieve Your Goals

Marketing is behind every product, every company, every movement, every person who achieves great things. Yet most of us are unknown outside of a small network of friends and professional contacts.

Many hardworking people are self-promotion challenged. I get it. No one likes a relentless self-promoter.

Nor do I. That's not what I'm advocating.

Let's assume the job market remains robust, in the spirit of positive thinking. But in a hybrid, remote, and in-person workplace that's increasingly global and technology driven, you still risk being left behind. Or being viewed as a commodity. Or being invisible. And that's never good.

Become a Little Bit Famous

That's why you should think of becoming *a little bit famous*.

We're talking here of becoming a little bit famous on *some level*—famous in your department, your company, your industry, your neighborhood, or the world—whatever your goals are.

We're talking of becoming a little bit famous *for something*—your positioning, an idea, a point of view, an area of expertise, a major project or achievement, an unusual skill or talent.

And we're talking about becoming a little bit famous *across multiple platforms*—your website and the social media platforms you're focusing on. Marketers think in terms of maximizing the number of touch points where a customer "touches" the brand, and you should too.

Marketing is everything you do to build visibility, awareness,
and engagement with your target market to achieve your goals

And we're talking about becoming a little bit famous *with a specific target audience* who is important in your success. You're not going after everybody, after all.

What's Your Q Score?

We're attracted to famous people, often just because they are famous. Being well known and well liked is important for a brand, whether it's a person or a product, and it's measured by the *Q Score* (or Q-Rating). Movie makers and marketers use the Q Score in deciding who to cast for a movie or commercial.

Interestingly, the Q Score is based on just two questions asked of thousands of people.[1] First: "Have you ever heard of person X?" This is the *familiarity score*. If someone says yes, they are asked the second question: "How would you rate the person?" The choices are: *poor, fair, good, very good, one of my favorites*. This is the *popularity score*. You get the Q Score by multiplying the familiarity score with the popularity score.

You probably can guess who has a high Q Score. Actors like Tom Hanks and Matt Damon, entertainers like Beyoncé and Taylor Swift, and athletes like Michael Jordan and Shaq O'Neill are not just famous; they're famous in a good way. They are well known and well liked by lots of people.

You've got a Q Score, too, but it's not the kind you can uncover from the company that does the survey. You can get a measure of your social media presence from various online tools or do your own sleuthing online. For example, you can check out how many people are checking out your profile on LinkedIn.

You'll find that your success increases the more visible you are in your company, your industry, social media, or whatever arena you're targeting. Likability is critical in your success, too. The work world is as much a personality contest as high school ever was.

Visibility is important because it has a halo effect. People will think you are better than others who are not well known or are invisible in your organization. "Sally must be better than Sam, or why else is she so well known?" is how the thinking goes.

That's why you need to become a little bit famous, beginning with one step at a time.

Personal Brand Visibility Ladder

It's hard to achieve your visibility goals all at once. You need a step-by-step approach.

- **Company recognition:** Most people begin branding by building a reputation internally as the company resident expert, leader of a team, or other positioning and expand their brand footprint from there. You can select one or two social media sites, like LinkedIn, for external brand building. Take advantage of company networking and industry networking events.
- **Regional or industry recognition:** As you expand your bandwidth, start to play an active role at industry meetings and conferences as a panelist or committee member. Volunteer to participate in regional or national projects at your company. Begin to build a stronger presence in social media platforms and at industry networking events.
- **National media recognition:** To build a broader reputation, you can explore international conferences, TED talks, media interviews, podcasts, blogs, and the like. This is the time to have a solid presence on a range of social media platforms. You can put together a media kit

or EPK (Electronic Press Kit) with your bio and a prepackaged set of promotional materials for journalists to write a story.

Think Like a Mini Media Mogul

In many ways, it's the best of times for personal branding. We're living in a time of opportunity when access to promoting on social media and the internet—*content marketing*—is democratic and available to all. In the pre-internet era, only celebrities, star athletes, and corporate icons had the PR apparatus to build a personal brand.

Now anyone with a smartphone and internet connection can do it. Everything you do and say can be captured on Instagram, YouTube, Twitter, LinkedIn, TikTok, and other social media. Influencers and internet mavens do it every day. Plus there are free and low-cost digital tools that can help you with marketing, too.

There's nothing to stop you from creating content and posting it wherever you like online. Except for the one thing that we are all short of—time.

That's why I say you've got to think like a mini media mogul and simplify the process or else you will be buried in content production and marketing activities.

Three Marketing Rules to Live By

Successful content marketing is about publishing content and building your visibility on a regular basis. Doing that well requires interacting, listening, and joining in the conversation.

The only way to do that, without content production taking over your life, is to be efficient, with a system in place. In short, you need the lazy person's guide to content marketing.

Follow these three shortcuts:

1. **Repurpose All Your Content:** Never write an article, make a video, or do a podcast without repurposing it into a series of *small media nuggets* for distribution on all your internet platforms.

Tip: Create a *Long Content log* to keep track of all your long-form articles, videos, interviews, and blog posts for repurposing into other formats such as quote cards, mini videos, tweets, etc. You can always tap into digital tools and freelance help for repurposing your existing content.

2. **Set Up a Content Development Pipeline:** As a media mogul, you need to capture ideas for future content development to keep the wheels of the content machine turning. It will save time to pick a preferred platform that you always use for developing original long-form content, whether it's video, audio, or text.

   Tip: Create a *Content Development folder* for news stories and ideas for future content. When you create new long-form content, send it through the repurposing process.

3. **Jump Into the Conversation and Trending Topics:** Another way to get your name out there without eating up too much time is to jump into existing social media conversations and use trending hashtags.

   Tip: Comment on other people's posts and respond to comments on your posts. Try to use trending hashtags on your content to take advantage of trending topics.

Create *How-To* Content

Ever wonder what people are doing all day long on their mobile phones? Chances are they are caught up in *micro-moments,* those sporadic impulses we all have throughout the day to learn something, do something, or discover something.

Micro-moments are important because they are *intent-rich moments* when decisions are made and information is gathered.[2] So it's perfect timing for someone to connect with you if you have a good website with helpful information and how-to videos on the topic.

As a personal brander, you want to maximize the chances you come up in these micro-moments. People are looking for information tailored to their needs. If you're an entrepreneur, think of the questions you're frequently asked. Whatever you do, what kind of how-to content can you put out there that people are interested in and need?

Micro-moments are all about being informative and quick, so make sure your website has good SEO (search engine optimization) and is *mobile optimized* so people don't have page-load issues on their mobile devices.

Share Your Two Cents

Your content strategy can be built around a point of view on important issues in your industry or job function or on issues completely outside the normal business conversation.

Your point of view could be on anything that you're passionate about—social, environmental, or moral issues. Focusing on a specific issue connects you with people—your target audience—who have a similar point of view.

Patagonia, the outdoor-clothing and gear brand, is well known for its bold eco-friendly point of view that resonates with its well-to-do, environmentally conscious customers. Its website is as much about living responsibly and all the things you can do "to keep your stuff in play as long as possible," as it is about selling clothes and gear.

In a world driven by moral standards, taking a stance on an issue of importance can be a powerful differentiator and way to connect with your target audience. Beware of a radical or contrary point of view. You may be practicing your right to free speech but busting your career.

The Grand Master of Content

To produce a lot of content on a regular basis, look at how the big names dominating the internet do it. One of most successful names in personal branding is business adviser Gary Vaynerchuk (aka Gary Vee), who advocates "Document" not "Create." The idea is to focus on documenting your journey, your thoughts, your process, and your progress, not on creating slick, new content from scratch every day.

He's also the master of repurposing. His "pillar content"—articles, vlog, interviews, books—is his foundation that he repackages into multiple small content bites. Everything is reused on a range of social media platforms and in different formats (videos, text, quote cards, pictures, memes).

Vaynerchuk is also the grand master of the hashtag, the # symbol that is used to group related tweets or messages together. Hashtags can help you read the pulse of what's happening so what you post is relevant in your community and in the world at large.

His formula is to look at Twitter's Top 30 trending hashtags. Try to figure out how to use three or so of the trending hashtags in your own pieces of content or storytelling.[3] Then post on social media to hop on the trend. You'll find that riding the trending wave is more effective at reaching people than creating a new hashtag and hoping it tops the trending list.

Create a Story Bank

Think of developing a story bank of personal and business stories for your *Story Toolbox* to use on social media, your website, talks, and meetings. Look for stories from your own experience, or stories you hear from colleagues that frame a specific incident or demonstrate a company or personal value.

Here are key stories you need to develop.

- **Origin Story:** Everyone needs an *origin story*. It's the story about how you became who you are and chose your career path. It's the story you use when people ask "How did you choose your career?" or "Tell me about yourself" or "How did you start your business?"
- **Redemption Story:** This is about a career or personal failure or even a crime, like the path to forgiveness of Nike executive Larry Miller. On the television show *Sixty Minutes,* Miller revealed that he had murdered a man when he was 16 years old and served prison time, a secret he had kept for over 50 years. It was a spellbinding story told with emotion, vulnerability, and courage.
- **Customer Story:** It could be about getting your first big client or a letter from a customer that demonstrates your commitment to resolving problems.
- **Quest Story:** Like *The Odyssey,* this story is about overcoming obstacles to achieve an important goal, so it's a perfect format for accomplishing difficult projects in the new world of work.

Use your stories to motivate your team, share with a customer, tell your boss, or as part of a job interview or new business pitch. In your stories, try to embed a memorable phrase or image that will be the takeaway from the story.

One "story" that can be hard to get is the *customer testimonial*. When you have a major accomplishment recognized by your boss or a client, that is the perfect time to pounce and ask for a testimonial. People are busy, so what I find works is to have a conversation and draft a short testimonial for their approval.

Underutilized Branding Tool: Your Bio

Many bios are a laundry list of job titles. That's a mistake. There's no branding in a laundry list.

A bio is not a resume. It's a narrative. The purpose of a bio is to define who you are, what's different about you, and intrigue people so they want to know more. Your bio should tell a story that ties together all the different aspects of your career and connects the dots with your brand positioning.

Remember, your bio doesn't have to include everything you've ever done. When you get bogged down in the past with multiple changes in direction, you confuse people. (Unless it's a narrative that shows how hard it was to find your purpose.) Your bio should lead people in the direction you are taking your career. Curate or deaccession things that are irrelevant to your career trajectory.

You'll also need to have variations of your bio, beginning with a short headline bio, important for the LinkedIn search algorithm. Use this valuable real estate to market your Unique Selling Proposition (USP) and career accomplishments. It should feature frequently searched, strategic keywords.

Your bio profile needs to be customized for each social media network. Some sites like Twitter and Instagram limit your profile to a few lines; others, like LinkedIn's summary or "About" section, give you the chance to tell your whole story.

Your Website and Long-Tail Keywords

If you're interested in personal branding, you need a personal website, ideally yourname.com. It's real estate you own, so you can control the content and design. You can feature your narrative bio, key accomplishments, testimonials, and blog.

Align your site with keywords and short phrases that people you're targeting—recruiters, colleagues, industry leaders, or customers, for example—might use to find someone like you.

There are *short-tail keywords*—one or two words that are broad in scope. Short-tail keywords will attract a lot of traffic but will be hard to stand out like "branding" or "lawyer."

What you need to focus on are *long-tail keywords*—short phrases that are more specific, like "personal branding speaker" or "bankruptcy lawyer." There will be less traffic, but also less competition, so you're more likely to be seen and found. Google suggestions are a good source of long-tail keywords.

Managing Up in the New World of Work

Working in tandem with your *external marketing* on social media and the internet is your *internal marketing campaign* so you're in the visibility loop at your company. Your boss should be the number-one person in your target audience if you work in a company.

If you're working remotely, or your boss is, achievements can be overlooked in the hybrid work space. It's your job to communicate your achievements, not your boss's job to ferret them out, as Naomi discovered.

Naomi led two successful projects during the height of the pandemic, yet when the list of new VPs was announced, Naomi was not on the list.

When she shared her disappointment, in light of the difficulty of her accomplishments, her boss told her, "Naomi, I didn't know you did all of those things. You never told me."

No one likes it when good people are overlooked because they struggle with marketing. But Naomi needed to realize that she must rethink not only how to manage her remote work, but how to manage up in the new world of work.

"Rich" vs. "Lean" Media

You may relish the freedom, sense of control, and efficiency you get in remote working and using Slack or email as your main communication vehicle. Plus, you don't have to deal with potentially awkward real-time interactions in person, on Zoom, or the phone.

> Some say face time is overrated.
> I say, "Avoid it at your peril."

According to Media Richness Theory, *rich media* like face-to-face in-person meetings or Zoom meetings have a tremendous advantage because you can hear someone's tone of voice, see their facial expressions, and watch their gestures and movements.[4]

In-person communication is a much "richer," nuanced experience for building engagement and nurturing relationships. It's real-time communication, so you can react directly to what's said.

Lean media like email and text have fewer visual or auditory clues, and a slower interaction rate. So it's a more detached way to communicate and can be a problem if you rely on it because people can misunderstand you or not feel connected to you.

Email is good, though, when precise information needs to be shared. Text plays an important role too. It has immediacy and signals urgency, and the recipient has the ability to respond quickly without a lengthier conversation.

Marketing with a Plan

Doing the tough strategic work is one thing. But it doesn't mean anything if you don't take action with a marketing plan with clear, specific tactics to achieve your goals.

Personal Brand Action Plan

- **Goals:** Set two or three concrete goals.
- **Target markets:** Specific people and groups you need to influence
- **Personal brand positioning and messaging:** Based on the work you did on the Top Ten Strategies, establish the positioning that best leverages your talents in the current marketplace and key topics to develop for content marketing.
- **Time frame:** Set a time frame to achieve your goals.
- **Tactics:** List three-to-five specific actions you will take to achieve your goals.
  - **Example:** If your goal is to assume more responsibility or become better in one aspect of your job, your action plan could include things like speaking to your boss about your goal; networking; expanding your skill set; volunteering for a project; taking a course to improve your skills; becoming involved on social media (like LinkedIn groups); and expanding your visibility on social media, etc.
- **Media platforms:** Specific social media, blog, podcasts, website, etc.
- **Metrics:** Measure your progress at specific time periods.

When Everything's On Brand

There was an inspiring moment on January 20, 2021, when the 22-year-old African American poet Amanda Gorman stepped into history on the steps of the United States Capitol as the youngest inaugural poet laureate.

In the blink of an eye, Gorman's show-stopping reading of her poem "The Hill We Climb" at the inauguration of President Joe Biden transformed her personal brand from a relatively under-the-radar poet to one of the most talked about people in the world.

In preparing her poem, she saw her task shift to a "cleansing by way of words" in the aftermath of the January 6 insurrection in Washington, DC.

The sentiments of Gorman's poem and her remarkable delivery made for *A Star is Born* moment.

The Whole Package

Gorman calls the oration of poetry an art form, and she sees language as the great connector. She uses clothes as part of her art, like the bright-yellow Prada coat and red hairband sitting like a tiara she wore for the inauguration.

She got everyone's attention not just because she's so young and an amazing wordsmith. She appears to be the real deal. She's a creative innovator—the youngest poet laureate—with a powerful message through poetry and a striking presence and delivery.

Branding Lessons Abound

One thing I have discovered is that anything is possible. This is true whether your goal is a complete brand overhaul, quitting your life-sucking job, or launching your own business.

Think of your goals. Brainstorm. Take baby steps first, then bigger steps, then leap. I've worked with individuals and with groups, large and small. It's amazing how goals can be achieved by following the branding process.

Chapter 17

Think in Terms of Emotional Engagement with Your Key Target Markets

Powerful brands touch people. Brands today are not about the product but about the relationship between the brand and the target market. That's why today's brand managers put a lot of emphasis on *emotional branding*, *brand personality*, *market segments*, and *total brand experience*.

We form the strongest bonds with brands we like, identify with, and feel emotionally connected with in our lives.

Think in Terms of Markets

Business success is built around relationships, too. Your success depends on what other people—your target markets—think of you. It doesn't matter who is "objectively" more qualified or talented. What matters is what the people making the decision feel about you and your abilities versus the other people you are competing with.

Think about all the people who are important to your brand—your boss, your clients, and your colleagues—in terms of target markets and follow these six rules of thumb.

Rule 1: Prioritize Your Target Markets

Most people make the mistake of defining the market too broadly.

In branding, markets are defined, segmented, and prioritized. No one has the resources or time to go after everyone. No brand can appeal to everybody. Neither can you. It's smart to pay more attention to the people who have the greatest impact on your brand's success. Think of your key target market as "customers" for Brand You. You want to create loyal customers by focusing on your most important customers.

Think in terms of primary and secondary markets:

- *Primary target market:* These are the key people who are the most important to your personal brand in helping you achieve your career and life goals.
- *Secondary target market:* These people also have some impact on your brand and could become more important in the future.

Rule 2: Create Loyal Customers

There's a saying in branding that you know a product has become a brand when your customers are your salespeople. That's why branders put so much focus on building a community among their customers. And they strengthen community ties through loyalty marketing programs or friendship branding with special events and rewards programs for customers.

To build a community of "loyal customers" for Brand You, you must understand what makes the people you are targeting tick.

If you were a competitor, how could you top your performance with your primary target market? What would your boss, colleagues, clients, and others in your primary target market love you to do that you are not doing now? Start doing it.

What are the sore spots? What are you doing that they don't like? Stop doing it.

What changes can you make to increase your target market's level of satisfaction?

The more precisely you define the needs and desires of the people in your target market, the easier it is to develop the best solutions, messages, and approaches to satisfy those needs and desires.

Rule 3: Develop a Clear Value Proposition

In analyzing market segments, you're looking for an opportunity. With which group would you be most successful? What is the right personal brand strategy for this target market? What is your value proposition—what do you have to offer them that competitors don't?

If the target market is defined too broadly, your value proposition won't resonate with anyone because it will be too broad and vague. It will be impossible to build a strong brand identity, too. Your image will be too general to attract interest and loyalty.

In attacking a narrow target market, you need to make sure the segment has enough size and growth potential. You want to own a valuable target market niche.

Say you are a financial consultant targeting women (Target Market Positioning Strategy No. 7). Which women are your best prospects? Women differ in age, income, education, lifestyle, marital status, geographic origin, and psychology.

Even women with high net worth may be too broad a target market. Maybe it's high-net-worth female executives and entrepreneurs. Or it could be women who are divorced or are planning to divorce. Or maybe it's widows. Or it could be women who have inherited money.

Each of these target markets has distinct needs and interests that would not be satisfied with an approach that targets the broader market of women in general.

Rule 4: Build an Emotional Bond

Today, brand managers put such a strong emphasis on emotional branding because people form the strongest relationships with brands they like and care about.

In branding and in the workplace, it's often the emotional ties that bind.

Rationally, we may be able to make a case for why the capabilities of one company are better than another's or why one person's experience is superior to that of another. Yet our gut may tell us something different. We choose the one that makes us feel more comfortable emotionally.

Your goal in personal branding is also to build satisfied and loyal customers, people who have good things to say about you because they have strong feelings about you, too.

One simple thing to keep in mind: listen more and talk less.

Listening seems so simple, yet few have mastered the art. Listening helps in building strong relationships and engaging your target audience.

When you listen rather than talk, you flatter your audience. You'll create a great impression (and learn a lot at the same time). When you listen, you are telling people that you think they are smart and worth listening to. You are saying that you care about their concerns, that you feel something for them. Listening also says that you are the type of person who wants to learn and improve.

It's so simple and so powerful. By simply listening, you often engage your target markets more profoundly than by saying something profound.

Rule 5: Think Outside-In

A cardinal rule of branding is to think first of what reaction you want from your target audience (outside), then figure out what you have to do to get that reaction (inside).

So don't begin with what you want (inside-out). Begin with what you want your target audience to do, then plan your action. For example, if you are a salesperson, the reaction you want, of course, is a sale. But if you go right into a sales message with a new client, you probably won't get the reaction you want. Most people don't want to be sold, but they do want to buy. A better tactic is to get to know what the client's needs are and avoid "selling."

Think in terms of *framing* your message. People are different and what would work with one sales prospect (or any target group) might be completely wrong for another. Frame your message and how you act so that you connect with people's wants and desires. You want to connect with their "bias," what's important and relevant to them.

Rule 6: Attract through "Soft Power"

The term "soft power" was coined by Joseph S. Nye in a book about how to attract people to your ideas in the arena of world politics. We're all familiar with exerting power through the carrot (paying someone) and the stick (threatening someone). Soft power is the third way. It uses things like your values, style, and point of view to attract others to you.

As I've said, branding shows you a lot about how to develop a style and point of view and other soft power ideas. One thing to think about that will increase your ability to attract others to you is executive presence. An important component of executive presence is bearing—the way you inhabit space. How do you enter a room? Do you stand tall and walk purposefully? Do you make an entrance? Or do you slouch and look distracted? Something as simple and controllable as bearing, your posture and stance and the way you move, is a powerful self-branding device that signals a lot to your target audience.

The other important component of executive presence is comportment—your way of conducting yourself when interacting with others. It's knowing how to greet and make conversation with new people at an industry event or Zoom call. It's knowing how to lead a meeting or handle an irate client. It's knowing how to behave in expected and unexpected situations, regardless of how many eyes are on you. It's knowing how to have an impact virtually when you're working remotely.

Now, let's look at the people in your target markets.

Guess Who's Number One?

If you work in a company, your boss is probably your number one target market.
Why?

Your boss has the most control over Brand You (unless you have an internal network that's better than your boss, or very loyal external clients, or are related to someone important).

Look at Zoe's story. Warm and engaging, Zoe had an impressive background in brand management at well-known packaged goods companies. Unfortunately, she had spent her career building brands for others and had not done much to build her brand. Here she was, in her early forties, unable to get to the next level although she had been with the same company for eight years. She worked hard and had a loyal team, yet some colleagues with similar experience and levels of responsibility had been promoted to vice president, two levels above her.

What was she doing wrong? Her problem was a familiar one: "The boss doesn't appreciate me." How did Zoe respond to her problem? She avoided her boss. She went remote! And she stayed remote even when her boss asked all direct reports to come in two days a week.

Do you think that was a good tactic for achieving her goal of being promoted to VP? (She was ignoring her primary target market.)

Think Truth or Consequences

Emotionally, I could understand why Zoe wanted to work remotely and avoid in person encounters. She was upset that she hadn't been promoted but her behavior was career sabotage. It was completely counterproductive to her goal of becoming a corporate VP.

Zoe had established a distant, formal relationship with her boss. Things were so bad that even pre-pandemic she was communicating with him primarily through e-mail and memos and as infrequently as possible.

Why hadn't Zoe been promoted?

In her performance evaluations, Zoe's boss gave her high marks in many areas but consistently low marks in leadership and communications skills. Her boss told her that she needed to play a stronger role in initiating projects, selling them to management, and increasing her visibility in the company.

Of course, Zoe felt that she had done all these things, often more than colleagues who had been promoted. After all, she had fifteen people reporting to her. But, her boss didn't perceive her as being a leader or having a high enough profile to be a VP.

Perception Is Everything

The business world, like most places, operates on *perceptions*.

It really didn't matter that Zoe supervised a larger group than many of her colleagues had. She was viewed as a weak brand and not a vice president brand. And, in most companies, if your boss doesn't nominate you for VP, you will not have those two letters appearing after your name no matter how good you are.

So, if this happens to you, the choice is clear: you must either change your boss's perceptions of you or find a new boss somewhere else.

Zoe was stuck in an outdated junior image.

Her task was to develop a self-brand action plan that would change people's perceptions so that Zoe would be seen as the leader she is. She needed to improve her communication and presentation skills and dramatically increase her visibility inside and outside the firm.

Take Action for a New Reaction

Above all, Zoe needed to stop avoiding her boss. She had to emotionally engage him in what she could do. She decided to adopt the hybrid work schedule.

To begin the process, she had to build rapport with her boss by meeting with him, making eye contact, and interacting in a more relaxed manner.

Rather than approach him as the "boss" or the "enemy," Zoe had to approach him as a trusted confidant (even as a friend). She needed to replace her negative self talk with a positive mantra ("My boss is my ally").

Zoe had to approach him as if he were the way she wanted him to be. Often, if we treat people in a certain way, they start behaving to match. If that didn't work, her plan B was to launch a job search.

Slay the Dragon

Zoe had to gain more confidence as a business presenter. She was great in front of her own team, but hated to present to her colleagues and senior executives. She hid behind a blizzard of PowerPoint bullets and spoke too fast to hide her nervousness.

Zoe told me that when she had to present to an important audience, her mind would go blank. The detailed slides were her safety net.

It turns out that Zoe had an inner critic, a voice inside her head that screamed, "You're not good enough" or "You'll forget something important and do a terrible job." It immobilized her and inhibited her performance.

The good news is that these feelings are common. I've had to fight an inner critic throughout my life, and many of my clients have had to as well. Here are some techniques to slay the inner critic:

- *Use positive self talk:* Talk back to your inner critic. Say, "That's not true. I *am* good enough!" One client even told me that she imagines her inner critic as a pesky crow on her shoulder who she shoos away.
- *Visualize a confident, successful you:* Many pro golfers are taught to visualize hitting the perfect shot as they approach the tee, even imagining exactly where the ball is going to land. Visualization can be powerful in business, too. It's like the avatar you might choose in an online game. I often visualize a poised, charismatic alter ego before I give a talk, and sometimes it even works!
- *Tune in to your body and your breathing:* Breathe deeply through your diaphragm, not shallowly through your upper chest. Even becoming aware of your body, of your feet firmly planted on the ground, can be a wonderful way to relax.
- *Have a pre-talk ritual:* Actors have a ritual that they go through before a stage performance. They do physical warm-up exercises, vocal exercises, visualizations, or they listen to a tape—whatever works to get them relaxed and ready to perform. Find your own ritual to get you in the zone.

Improve What You Can

Zoe also worked on slowing down her rapid-fire speech. She spoke so fast that I often had to replay her voice-mail messages to decipher them!

One of the first things she did was join Toastmasters. After she gained some experience with that group, she offered to give a talk at a local university in order to develop more confidence in her presentation skills. She upgraded her business casual wardrobe.

Little by little, Zoe started getting a different response from her boss and others at her company as she became a better communicator. She also increased her visibility within the company by volunteering to lead an important strategic initiative.

When Zoe's boss selected her to represent him at an important company-wide meeting in Europe, she knew she had turned the corner. (And Zoe did get her happy ending. She made VP, and the company even added a new group to her department.)

Offer Something Competitors Don't

Whatever your target market, you'll want to have a personal brand strategy that provides a compelling value proposition, a reason to choose you over your competitors. That's why the Top 10 Personal Branding Strategies can be so helpful.

One client, Kat, had a long career in video production and wanted to start her own business. The problem was that the video production category was crowded. How could she standout?

So she focused on a narrow segment of the market where she had special expertise: training videos for cosmetics companies. But there were some entrenched competitors here as well. After she took the online Personal Brand Finder assessment test, she came up with a compelling positioning idea.

Kat had some special attributes that set her apart and formed the core of her strategy. She was a woman (and could provide a woman's touch) in the video production business, which was dominated by men. She had a long history of producing high-end videos for top cosmetics brands. She knew how to get the lighting, makeup, and staging for top production values.

Kat also had a hidden asset. Before becoming a video producer, she had been a television morning show host Bingo! She had a winning strategy: strong on both sides of the camera. She had a unique heritage (Heritage Strategy No. 9).

Defining her business proposition this way dramatically improved the power of Kat's concept compared to those of her competitors. The value to clients was high-end know-how, whether they were preparing a video for their business or a media push that required someone to do a great job looking good in the public eye. Her unique heritage was a different idea, and one that resonated with her target audience.

Kat was able to tie together her assets: her strong client contacts, experience with some of the world's top cosmetics brands, experience as a television host, and a woman's touch to offer clients a clear value proposition.

Find Your Super Power

Like empathy, intuition is a powerful tool in business for making decisions, analyzing problems, and building relationships. An ad executive at a major global ad agency, Tara was known for her ability to psyche out her clients. Tara had the uncanny ability to unlock the *hidden agenda*—what clients really want but don't articulate—that can make the difference between success and failure in business.

Tara was great at reading body language in meetings. Once, an important prospect said very little as the meeting proceeded with its agenda. Tara sensed that something was amiss, and she wondered, "Gee, I think we missed something. Should I bring it up?" At the end of the meeting she said, "Before you make your decision, I would like to meet with you and show you one of our other proposals. In hindsight, I think it might fit your needs better."

It's amazing, but that exchange led to a close business relationship between Tara and the client. Afterward, Tara's colleagues at the company told her, "You have just added more value than we could have in building a relationship with this client." The important thing is to have the courage to act on your intuition when you feel something strongly.

Don't Underestimate the Importance of Likeability

Whether we like it or not, business is a popularity contest as much as high school ever was, just without the spit balls.

Brand personality is am important differentiator for a brand. And for you too.

Unlike with a product, you don't need to manufacture a brand personality. You've got a unique personality. You'll find the road to success much easier if you are perceived as likeable, as someone others want to have on the team. Especially in markets like today's where there is a lot of choice, having a likeable personality can spell the difference between success and failure. Here are five general principles you can use to influence your likeability:

1. *The Attractiveness Principle:* We have already discussed the importance of visual identity in personal branding. Attractiveness influences that all-important first impression. It has a halo effect and leads to a lot of positive assumptions. And we can all put ourselves together to be attractive.

2. *The Similarity Principle:* Finding common ground or relevance is a good networking and branding tool, and it also influences likeability. We like people who are similar to us in some way, whether it is in personality, lifestyle, political beliefs, or an old school tie.

3. *The Empathy Principle:* The best way to get someone to like you is to like them. Put the focus on others. Empathize with them, and they will like you. Be careful of how you criticize others in the virtual world where criticism can come across as harsh without the nuance of the personal touch.

4. *The Familiarity Principle:* We like people with whom we are familiar and have contact, whether it's through personal contact, via the media, or by reputation. That's why visibility is important for people and brands.

5. *The Authenticity Principle:* Authenticity may be the cardinal rule of branding. You have to be yourself, not try to be someone else or fulfill other people's expectations and values. Being comfortable in your own skin is powerful.

Tom Hanks ranks high on most people's likeability meter. What makes him so likeable? Hanks is nice-looking, so he fulfills the Attractiveness Principle. But he's not too attractive, so he also taps into the Similarity Principle. Both his public and movie personae suggest that he is someone we could relate to, who treats others well, satisfying the Empathy Principle.

Hanks also fulfills the Familiarity Principle. Movies have made him famous and familiar. Many celebrities share their stories, experiences, and values through the media. Fans feel that they know the celebrity and often become emotionally involved in that person's life.

Above all, Hanks seems to be a regular guy. He seems open and unaffected, which fulfills the Authenticity Principle. He appears to be comfortable in his own skin. He seems like someone you could get to know and someone you would want to be. In a word, Hanks is likeable.

It's Up to You

We've been on an exciting journey together. You've learned a lot about brand positioning strategy, including the Top Ten Brand Positioning Strategies from the commercial world of brands.

You've learned the importance of understanding the needs and perceptions of your target market. You've selected the best way to position Brand You based on your unique gifts and the needs in the current marketplace. We've focused on visual identity, verbal identity, and brand personality, and tactics for marketing Brand You to achieve your goals.

Make It Your Best Life

Now you know what the personal branding path requires of you. What happens next is up to you. Life is too short for the wrong career. Your brand is too important to leave to chance.

We're living in a dynamic era—a new world of work—continuously evolving through technology and change.

Nobody knows how things will play out in the future. There will be times for bold actions and personal branding advances, and times for sitting still and assessing, and times for reinvention.

Whether you're competing in a corporation or as an entrepreneur, you must become fluent in personal branding, particularly in the new world of work. You must know how to create a personal brand and how to market it. Expressing your truest personal brand is the ultimate competitive advantage, not just for career success, but for life success.

Personal branding is the journey of a lifetime. Your goal is to live the life you want. Enjoy it.

Acknowledgments

This book started with a question. What's the key to succeeding in life as well as your career in today's new world of work?

Answering that question involved research but also a lot of listening. I wish I could thank every person who gave me their insights, observations and experiences on the front lines in today's increasingly digital, remote and hybrid workplace. (To protect the privacy of interviewees, I've used pseudonyms when I've shared their stories.) Thank you one and all.

To Gary Andrew Gulkis, my mentor, toughest critic and writing guru, I am ridiculously grateful to you for your suggestions for improving the book. Thanks for always being willing to do one more reading of the manuscript.

To Al Ries, my first boss in advertising who's now in the Marketing Hall of Fame, thank you for the solid grounding in positioning and brand strategy that underpins this book.

I want to thank Dr. Ren Li, who helped with the development of the online Personal Brand Assessment Test.

To Holly Bennion as well as Melissa Carl, Michelle Surianello and the team at Nicholas Brealey who supported the book from the beginning and shepherded it through the publishing process at a swift pace. Thanks so much.

A big thank you to my partner Mike and our son, Ramsey, who had to put up with more takeout food than I'd like to admit as I worked on the book throughout the pandemic. My book project gave me a purpose through this difficult time as the pandemic stretched from one year to the next. And for that I am grateful.

Finally, I want to thank you, my reader.

Notes

Introduction

1. Patrick Van Kessel and Laura Silver, "Where Americans Find Meaning in Life Has Changed Over the Past Four Years," Pew Research Center, November 18, 2021, https://www.pewresearch.org/fact-tank/2021/11/18/where-americans-find-meaning-in-life-has-changed-over-the-past-four-years/.

Chapter 1

1. Jeffrey A. Trachtenberg, "Who Wants to Hear Ralph Nader Praising CEOs? Not Publishers," *The Wall Street Journal,* March 1, 2022, https://www.wsj.com/articles/who-wants-to-hear-ralph-nader-praising-ceos-not-publishers-11646146420.

Chapter 2

1. Kim Parker, et al., "Covid-19 Pandemic to Reshape Work in America," Pew Research Center, February 16, 2022, https://www.pewresearch.org/social-trends/2022/02/16/covid-19-pandemic-continues-to-reshape-work-in-america/.
2. Christopher Shea, "The Great Pandemic Work-from-Home Experiment Was a Remarkable Success," *The Washington Post,* October 14, 2021, https://www.washingtonpost.com/outlook/the-great-pandemic-work-from-home-experiment-was-a-remarkable-success/2021/10/14/c21123d0-2c64-11ec-985d-3150f7e106b2_story.html.
3. "World Happiness Report 2021," Sustainable Development Solutions Network, accessed March 1, 2022, https://worldhappiness.report/ed/2021/.
4. Ian Cook, "Who Is Driving the Great Resignation?" *Harvard Business Review,* September 15, 2021, https://hbr.org/2021/09/who-is-driving-the-great-resignation.
5. "Business Formation Statistics," US Census Bureau, accessed March 1, 2022, https://www.census.gov/econ/bfs/index.html.
6. John Caplan, "The US Is Experiencing a Microbusiness Renaissance—Here's What It Looks Like," *Forbes,* May 21, 2021, https://www.forbes.com/sites/johncaplan

/2021/05/21/the-us-is-experiencing-a-microbusiness-renaissance-heres-what-it-looks
-like/?sh=1a1c1fb31c8d.

7. Catherine Morris and Sarah Feldman, "The Pandemic Inspired 1 in 5 Americans
to Reevaluate Their Lives," *Ipsos*, October 5, 2021, https://www.ipsos.com/en-us
/news-polls/pandemic-inspired-1-5-americans-reevaluate-their-lives#2.

8. Jane Thier, "95% of Knowledge Workers Want Flexible Hours More Than Hybrid
Work, and Managers Should Pay Attention," *Fortune,* February 3, 2022, https://fortune
.com/2022/02/03/knowledge-workers-say-they-want-flexible-hours-more-than-hybrid
-work/.

9. Sam Tayan, "Hybrid Workplaces: A Win-Win Solution for Business and Their
Employees in the New Normal," *Entrepreneur,* March 9, 2021, https://www.entre
preneur.com/article/366675.

10. Yang, Lonqi, et al., "The Effects of Remote Work on Collaboration Among
Information Workers," *Nature Human Behavior,* September 2021, https://www
.microsoft.com/en-us/research/publication/the-effects-of-remote-work-on-colla
boration-among-information-workers/.

11. Elizabeth Dilts Marshall, "Working from Home Doesn't Work for Those Who Want
to Hustle: JPMorgan CEO," Reuters, May 4, 2021, https://www.reuters.com/article
/us-jp-morgan-ceo/working-from-home-doesnt-work-for-those-who-want-to-hustle
-jpmorgan-ceo-idUSKBN2CL1HQ.

12. Peter Cappelli, "In a Hybrid Office, Remote Workers Will Be Left Behind," *The Wall
Street Journal,* August 13, 2021, https://www.wsj.com/articles/hybrid-workplace
-promotions-11628796072.

13. Greg Lewis, "Women and Gen Z Are More Likely to Apply to Remote Jobs,"
LinkedIn, February 12, 2021, https://www.linkedin.com/pulse/women-gen-z-more
-likely-apply-remote-jobs-linkedin-data-greg-lewis/.

14. Chip Cutter, "The Off-Site Is the New Return to the Office," *The Wall Street Journal,* February 5, 2022, https://www.wsj.com/articles/the-off-site-is-the-new-return
-to-the-office-11644057003.

15. Danielle Kost, "You're Right. You Are Working Longer and Attending More Meetings," Harvard Business School, September 14, 2020, https://hbswk.hbs.edu/item
/you-re-right-you-are-working-longer-and-attending-more-meetings.

16. *Contingent Work Force: Size, Characteristics, Earnings and Benefits*, April 20, 2015,
prepared by the US Government Accountability Office, https://www.gao.gov
/assets/670/669899.pdf.

17. "Workforce 2020," *Oxford Economics*, accessed February 25, 2020, https://www
.oxfordeconomics.com/workforce2020.

18. Robyn Vinter, "Over Three-Quarters of Britons Re-evaluate Their Lives During
Covid," *The Guardian,* July 11, 2021, https://www.theguardian.com/world/2021
/jul/12/over-three-quarters-britons-re-evaluate-lives-covid.

Chapter 3

1. "Volvo," *Ad Age*, September 15, 2003, https://adage.com/article/adage-encyclopedia
   /volvo/98923.
2. "The Future of Work After Covid-19," McKinsey Global Institute, February 18, 2021,
   https://www.mckinsey.com/featured-insights/future-of-work/the-future-of-work
   -after-covid-19.
3. Synchronous vs. Asynchronous Communication: The 2022 Guide, Get Guru.com,
   accessed March 1, 2022, https://www.getguru.com/reference/synchronous-vs-asyn
   chronous-communication.

Chapter 4

1. Steve Denning, "What's Behind Warby Parker's Success?" *Forbes*, March 23, 2016,
   https://www.forbes.com/sites/stevedenning/2016/03/23/whats-behind-warby
   -parkers-success/.
2. https://www.redbull.com/us-en/energydrink/history-of-red-bull, accessed February
   10, 2022.
3. Reid Hoffman, "5 Steps to Finding Your Next Big Idea from Spanx's Sara Blakely,"
   Medium, May 3, 2016, https://reid.medium.com/5-steps-to-finding-your-next-big
   -idea-from-spanxs-sara-blakely-9bb2b3b7b491.

Chapter 5

1. Joseph Epstein, "A Pollster Would Have Spiked the Gettysburg Address," *The Wall
   Street Journal,* October 26, 2021, https://www.wsj.com/articles/a-pollster-would
   -have-spiked-the-gettysburg-address-polling-public-opinion-11635279985.
2. Tim Ott, "How George Washington's Personal and Physical Characteristics Helped
   Him Win the Presidency," *Biography,* February 7, 2020, https://www.biography.com
   /news/george-washington-character-presidency.
3. Edelman Trust Barometer 2021, https://www.edelman.com/sites/g/files/aatuss191
   /files/2021-03/2021%20Edelman%20Trust%20Barometer.pdf.
4. Hannah L. Miller, "Mary Barra: From Co-Op Student Employee to GM's CEO," *Leaders,* January 25, 2022, https://leaders.com/articles/women-in-business/mary-barra/.
5. Amelia Lester, "The Roots of Jacinda Ardern's Extraordinary Leadership After
   Christchurch," *New Yorker,* March 23, 2019, https://www.newyorker.com/culture
   /culture-desk/what-jacinda-arderns-leadership-means-to-new-zealand-and-to
   -the-world?source=search_google_dsa_paid&gclid=Cj0KCQiAjc2QBhDgARIs
   AMc3SqTGRn0h9xOiyPqm507Wm9DNu1XrO_HNOdxhnejgbhYyoslzmyQajn
   gaAvE5EALw_wcB.

6. Max Nisen, "Male CEOs with Deeper Voices Run Bigger Companies And Make More Money," *Business Insider,* April 19, 2013, https://www.businessinsider.com /voice-pitch-and-success-2013-4.

7. David Robson, "The Reason Why Women's Voices Are Deeper Today," BBC, June 12, 2018, https://www.bbc.com/worklife/article/20180612-the-reasons-why -womens-voices-are-deeper-today.

8. Cockerell, Michael, "How the Iron Lady Changed Her Voice," BBC, https://www.bbc .co.uk/programmes/p00n3mr1.

Chapter 6

1. Jillian D'Onfro, "The Best Steve Jobs Quotes from his New Biography, which Apple Says Is the Best Depiction of Him Yet," *Business Insider,* May 24, 2015, https://www .businessinsider.com/steve-jobs-quotes-from-becoming-steve-jobs-2015-3.

2. Lillian Cunningham, "Richard Bronson: Virgin Stunt Man," *The Washington Post,* September 26, 2014, https://www.washingtonpost.com/news/on-leadership/wp /2014/09/26/richard-branson-virgins-stunt-man.

3. Avery Hartmans, "Elon Musk's Life Story," *Business Insider,* October 21, 2021, https://www.businessinsider.com/the-rise-of-elon-musk-2016-7.

Chapter 7

1. A. G. Lafley, "What P&G Learned from the Diaper Wars," *Fast Company,* February 26, 2012, https://www.fastcompany.com/3005640/what-pg-learned-diaper-wars.

2. "Pampers: The Birth of P&G's First 10-Billion-Dollar Brand," *P&G blog,* June 26, 2012, https://us.pg.com/blogs/pampers-birth-pgs-first-10-billion-dollar -brand/.

3. Emma Fraser, "What *Being the Ricardos* Gets Right (and Wrong) About Lucille Ball's Trailblazing Story," *Elle,* December 23, 2021, https://www.elle.com/culture /movies-tv/a38591374/is-being-the-ricardos-accurate-lucille-ball-fact-fiction/.

4. *Being the Ricardos,* movie, 2021.

5. Melody Wilding, "Why Groundedness Is the New Key to Success," *Forbes,* September 13, 2021, https://www.forbes.com/sites/melodywilding/2021/09/13/why-groundedness-is -the-new-key-to-success/?sh=4e940a816123.

Chapter 8

1. Gregory Zuckerman, "A Shot to Save the World," *The Wall Street Journal,* October 23, 2021, https://www.wsj.com/articles/theunlikelyoutsiders-who-won-the-race -for-a-covid-19-vaccine-ugur-sahin-stephane-bancel-moderna-biontech-11634932219.

2. Anneta Konstantinides, "Ina Garten Says She Quit Her White House Job to Buy a Grocery Shop at the Age of 30 Thanks to Advice from Her Husband," *Insider,* October 21, 2020, https://www.insider.com/ina-garten-left-white-house-job-became -famous-cook-2020-10.

3. "History of Toothpaste," Crest, accessed January, 2022, https://crest.com/en-us /oral-care-tips/toothpaste/history-toothpaste.

4. "Colgate vs. Crest," adbrands.net, accessed September 11, 2021, https://www .adbrands.net/archive/us/crest-us-p.htm

5. Lewis Braham, "How Jack Bogle Changed Investing," *Barron's,* January 18, 2019, https://www.barrons.com/articles/how-jack-bogle-changed-investing-51547769600.

Chapter 9

1. Michael Specter, "How Anthony Fauci Became America's Doctor," *New Yorker,* April 10, 2020, https://www.newyorker.com/magazine/2020/04/20/how-anthony -fauci-became-americas-doctor.

2. Michael Miller, "Busting the Myth of the 10,000 Hour Rule," *sixsecond,* accessed April 22, 2022, https://www.6seconds.org/2020/01/25/10000-hour-rule.

3. Richard Feloni, "Barbara Corcoran Says Standing Up to Donald Trump 30 Years Ago Was a Pivotal Moment in Her Life," *Business Insider,* November 7, 2016, https://www.businessinsider.com/barbara-corcoran-donald-trump-pivotal-mo ment-2016-11.

4. Michelle Fox, "How to Invest Like Warren Buffett," CNBC, September 19, 2019, https://www.cnbc.com/2019/09/19/heres-how-to-invest-like-warren-buffett.html.

Chapter 10

1. Heather Haddon, "TikTok Fans Brew Even More Complicated Orders at Star-bucks," *The Wall Street Journal,* November 4, 2021, https://www.wsj.com/articles /tiktok-fans-brew-even-more-complicated-orders-at-starbucks-11636049272.

2. Gloria Allred, accessed December 10, 2021, https://www.gloriaallred.com.

3. *Seeing Allred,* Netflix documentary, 2018.

4. Michael Fertik, "Why is Influencer Marketing Such a Big Deal Right Now?" Forbes, July 2, 2002, https://www.forbes.com/sites/michaelfertik/2020/07/02/why -is-influencer-marketing-such-a-big-deal-right-now/?sh=4e0d493675f3.

Chapter 11

1. Jacob Gallagher, "How 'Succession' Stoked a Frenzy for Status Baseball Caps," *The Wall Street Journal,* December 15, 2021, https://www.wsj.com/articles/succes sion-morning-show-luxury-baseball-caps-11639583315.

2. Lisa Trei, "Price Changes the Way People Experience Wines Study Shows," Stanford University, January 16, 2008, https://news.stanford.edu/news/2008/january16/wine-011608.html.
3. Chris Barilla, "Yeezy Gap x Balenciaga: A Look at Kanye's New Collab," *Distractify*, February 23, 2022, https://www.distractify.com/p/yeezy-gap-balenciaga-collab.

Chapter 12

1. "Absolut Vodka Unveils Its Biggest Design Update Since Launch in 1979," News, Absolute, accessed January 5, 2022, https://www.absolut.com/us/news/articles/new-bottle-design/.
2. Tracy Moore, "Here's to *Yellowstone*, the Most-Watched Show Everyone Isn't Talking About," *Vanity Fair,* November 5, 2021, https://www.vanityfair.com/hollywood/2021/11/yellowstone-season-4-paramount-plus.
3. Ashley Collman, "A College Counselor Told Michelle Obama She Wasn't Princeton Material—But She Applied Anyway and Got In," *Business Insider,* January 17, 2019, https://www.businessinsider.com/michelle-obama-wasnt-princeton-material-college-counselor-told-her-2018-11.

Chapter 13

1. *RBG,* directed by Julie Cohen and Betsy West, 2018, on Amazon Prime, https://www.amazon.com/RBG-Ruth-Bader-Ginsburg/dp/B07CT9Q5C6/ref=sr_1_1?crid=2J7UZ5VYM99Y3&keywords=rbg+documentary&qid=1645564748&s=instant-video&sprefix=rbg%2Cinstant-video%2C321&sr=1-1.
2. Elizabeth A. Harris, "Inside Kim Kardashian's Prison-Reform Machine," *The New York Times,* April 2, 2020, https://www.nytimes.com/2020/04/02/arts/television/kim-kardashian-prison-reform.html.

Chapter 14

1. Richard Thompson Ford, "How the Laws of Fashion Made History," *Medium,* February 2022, https://ourford.medium.com/how-the-laws-of-fashion-made-history-27df0ed4c270.
2. Suzanne Kapner, "You're Finally Going Back to the Office. What Are You Going to Wear?" *The Wall Street Journal,* June 4, 2019, https://www.wsj.com/articles/youre-finally-going-back-to-the-office-what-are-you-going-to-wear-11622799041.
3. Vanessa Friedman, "Kyrsten Sinema's Style Keeps Us Guessing," *The New York Times,* October 18, 2021, https://www.nytimes.com/2021/10/18/style/kyrsten-sinema-style.html.
4. Wanda Thibodeaux, "Being Successful Could Come Down to Changing Up Your Hair, Says Science," *Inc.,* accessed January 31, 2022, https://www.inc.com/wanda

-thibodeaux/being-successful-could-come-down-to-changing-up-your-hair-according -to-science.html.

5. Adwoa Bagalini, "How Wearing Natural Hairstyles Harms the Job Prospects of Black Women," World Economic Forum, February 11, 2021, https://www.weforum.org /agenda/2021/02/natural-hair-black-women-job-discrimination/.

6. Catherine Clifford, "Billionaire Jack Dorsey's 11 'Wellness' Habits: From No Food All Weekend to Ice Baths, CNBC.com, April 8, 2019, https://www.cnbc .com/2019/04/08/twitter-and-square-ceo-jack-dorsey-on-his-personal-wellness-hab its.html.

7. Vanessa Friedman, "What to Wear in the Metaverse," *The New York Times,* January 20, 2022, https://www.nytimes.com/2022/01/20/style/metaverse-fashion.html.

8. Heather Wilde, "Studies Prove That Power Posing Doesn't Work. Here's What to Do Instead," *Inc.,* October 30, 2019, https://www.inc.com/heather-wilde/studies -prove-that-power-posing-doesnt-work-heres-what-to-do-instead.html.

9. Vanessa Friedman, "The Verdict on the Elizabeth Holmes Trial Makeover," *The New York Times,* December 17, 2021, https://www.nytimes.com/2021/12/17/style/eliza beth-holmes-trial-makeover.html.

10. Vanessa Friedman, "The Man in the Olive Green Tee," *The New York Times,* March 21, 2022, file:///Users/catherine/Desktop/Book_Zerensky_Olive%20Green %20Tee%20-%20The%20New%20York%20Times.html.

Chapter 15

1. Helen Evans, "Science Explains Why Having a Deep Voice Is Critical to Our Success," Lifehack, accessed July 8, 2021, https://www.lifehack.org/372669/science -explains-why-having-deep-voice-critical-our-success-2.

2. Sue Shellenbarger, "The Sound of Your Voice Speaks Volumes," *The Wall Street Journal,* April 24, 2013, https://www.wsj.com/articles/BL-ATWORKB-894.

3. Kathryn O'Shea-Evans, "The New Secret to Online Dating Success? Your Voice," *The Wall Street Journal,* February 2, 2022, https://www.wsj.com/articles /online-dating-voice-notes-11643829216.

4. Jelena Djorkjevic, "A Rose by Any Other Name: Would It Smell as Sweet?" *The Journal of Neurophysiology,* January 2008, https://pubmed.ncbi.nlm.nih.gov/17959740/.

5. K. Aleisha Fellers, "Latest WTF Study: Your First Name Affects Your Love Life," *Women's Health,* February 17, 2015, https://www.womenshealthmag.com /relationships/a19898929/online-dating-screen-names/.

6. Hannah Poukish and Alex Cohen, "Research Shows Teachers Have Racial Biases When Grading Students' Work," Spectrum News 1, May 7, 2021, https:// spectrumnews1.com/ca/la-west/inside-the-issues/2021/05/07/research-shows -teachers-have-racial-biases-when-grading-students--work.

7. Julie Jargon, "College Students Have to Learn How to Make Small Talk," *The Wall Street Journal*, February 12, 2022, https://www.wsj.com/articles/college-students -forgot-how-to-talk-to-each-other-11644627316.

Chapter 16

1. Ethan Trex, "How Are Q Scores Calculated?" mentalfloss.com, April 12, 2011, https://www.mentalfloss.com/article/27489/how-are-q-scores-calculated.
2. Jonathan LaCoste, "WTF Is Micro-Moment Marketing?" *Inc.*, January 22, 2016, https://www.inc.com/jonathan-lacoste/wtf-is-micro-moment-marketing.html.
3. Gary Vaynerchuk, "How to Use Hashtags Correctly: A Guide to Every Social Network," accessed January 10, 2022, https://www.garyvaynerchuk.com/how-to -use-hashtags-correctly-a-guide-to-every-social-network/.
4. "Media Richness Theory," Mass Communication, Communication Theory, accessed December 5, 2021, https://www.communicationtheory.org/media-richness-theory/.

Index

About the Author

Image Courtesy of Dan Demetriad

Catherine Kaputa is an award-winning author, keynote speaker, and personal branding guru. Catherine has given branding presentations and conducted employee workshops at many of today's most innovative companies such as Google, Microsoft, PepsiCo, Intel, Merck, Unilever, and Citi.

Originally trained as an art historian in Asian art at Harvard, Catherine decided to leave her position at the Seattle Art Museum to follow her dream of living in New York City and being part of the dramatic changes taking place in the world of marketing and advertising. Catherine's hard work and branding expertise led her to become the management supervisor of the iconic "I Love New York" ad campaign that's copied today the world over. For over ten years, Catherine was SVP, Director of Advertising and Brand at Citi Smith Barney and has been named one of the top thirty branding gurus in the world.

Catherine is the author of *You Are a Brand*, currently translated into over ten languages as well as the founder of selfbrand.com dedicated to helping people use personal branding insights to achieve career success, personal fulfillment and happiness.

selfbrand.com   catherinekaputa.com   catherine@selfbrand.com